The End of American Literature

The End of American Literature

Essays from the Late Age of Print

Jeffrey R. Di Leo

Library of Congress Cataloging-in-Publication Data

Names: Di Leo, Jeffrey R., author.

Title: The end of American literature : essays from the late age of print / by Jeffrey R. Di Leo.

Description: Huntsville, Texas : Texas Review Press, [2019] |

Identifiers: LCCN 2019003199 (print) | LCCN 2019005394 (ebook) | ISBN 9781680031799 (eBook) | ISBN 9781680031782 | ISBN 9781680031782(pbk. :alk. paper)

Subjects: LCSH: Books and reading—Technological innovations—United States. | Book industries and trade—United States—History—21st century. | American literature. | American literature—Philosophy. | LCGFT: Essays.

Classification: LCC Z1003.2 (ebook) | LCC Z1003.2 .A6 2019 (print) | DDC 810.9—dc23

LC record available at https://lccn.loc.gov/2019003199

. . . it is the cursed inventions of the age that ruin everything—artillery, serpentines, bombards, and, above all, printing, that other pestilence from Germany. No more manuscripts! no more books! Printing is cutting up the bookselling trade. The end of the world is certainly at hand.

—Victor Hugo, *The Hunchback of Notre-Dame* (1831)

A book is a machine to think with, but it need not, therefore usurp the functions either of the bellows or the locomotive. This book might better be compared to a loom on which it is supposed to re-weave some raveled parts of our civilization.

—I. A. Richards, *Principles of Literary Criticism* (1924)

The book is like the wheel . . . once invented, it cannot be bettered.

—Umberto Eco in Jean-Claude Carrière and Umberto Eco, *This Is Not the End of the Book: A Conversation* (2012)

Contents

Preface

Every month now I get the same email. And this month was no different. It comes from a guy in New York City whose job it is publicize the books put out by his company. He works for a major book publisher with some incredible authors and titles, and he is one of their vice-presidents.

Unlike most of the other publicists that contact me by email, he does not make an effort to pretend that he knows me. There is no salutation like "Dear X." His email just gets down to the business of reporting upcoming titles without any acknowledgment as to the identity of his reader—and I like this aspect of it. I don't know him—and he doesn't know me—so why pretend any different?

In a way, this email is of a class with the others I regularly receive promoting new titles—and like 99 percent of these unsolicited emails, it too gets about 1 percent of my attention. If I have time, I might scroll through it. If I don't, it just gets deleted without reading. But an aspect of this recurring email has come to haunt my thoughts of late. It is contained in the last two lines of the "signature file" at the end of every update he sends me. It reads as follows:

> Seasonal catalogues are no longer being printed, but digital versions can be accessed at any time directly from our Media Center. To download the current listing, click on the link below.

I have thought about "click[ing] on the link" but just have not yet done so. Something about doing it stops me. It is his use of the words "are no longer being printed, *but* . . . ." But *what*? But the book world is shifting from a print-dominated one to a digitally dominated one. And book catalogs are now part of that transition.

Clicking that link has come to feel like a vote "for" this transition. And each month I am given another opportunity to elect the digital. I know it is not really a "vote" for the digital and that it is just a link to a catalogue, but having it offered to me monthly as not merely an alternative to the printed catalogue but as a replacement for it triggers a nerve.

It reminds me of the catalogues from this publisher that I used to receive several times a year, but which have now been digitally replaced. I start to wonder: will their books be next? Will this VP soon be sending me an email with the signature file "*Books* are no longer being printed, but digital versions can be accessed at any time directly from our Media Center"? Is clicking on the link *also* a vote for digital books only?

Next to my computer are piles of printed seasonal catalogs received from publishing houses across the country. They range from the phonebook-sized catalogues of the large, well-funded presses to the pamphlet-sized ones of the under-funded micropresses.

Some are elaborate works of graphic art, printed on high-quality paper with several pages devoted to their featured titles. I enjoy browsing them because of their high print quality and their amazing design work—with the best of them rivaling museum catalogues.

Other catalogs though are not much more than printed listings of new and forthcoming titles, the least elegant of which devoting nothing more than a line or two to the title, author, page count, ISBN, and price. The difference in their production quality from the "museum-quality" catalogs of other presses is usually reflected in a difference in the power and prestige of the press—but an email has changed everything. Now one of the most prestigious and influential publishers in America is asking us to "click on the link" rather than open their glossy catalog.

As a journal editor, the experience of reviewing these catalogs has become a ritualized one for me—something to which I look forward to in the fall, spring, and summer seasons. However, the piles of catalogs have been noticeably getting smaller each year with more and more publishers opting to only make them available digitally. Some only send print catalogs if requested, otherwise they too ask us for a link click.

The idea of getting your audience to digitally go to you rather than you materially going to them is a change in marketing direction for book publishers. One only possible at a time when digital catalogs can be made available to anyone who wants to access them—and printed catalogs are largely regarded as superfluous. The problem though is that not everyone is sold on the idea of digital catalogs. This is obvious because print catalogs are still being produced and distributed—evidenced by the large pile on my desk.

This is part of the uniqueness of our times. A time that is oddly enough captured, well—of all places—in the email signature line of a publicity executive from New York.

It is the late age of print. A time caught between the passing of one media age to another—the passing from the age of print to the digital age—and back again. A time when one day it seems like printed books and bookstores are on the decline, whereas on another it is ebooks (viz., "electronic" books) and the digital utopia showing signs of slippage. The dynamics between print and digital culture changing with respect to literature, books, and scholarship so frequently that tracking them is like chasing a tornado.

If there is one feeling that is common within the late age of print, it is that something might be ending—not that something is beginning. At the macrolevel, it can be seen in our prognostications about capitalism, democracy, and America. But though the essays herein draw on these broader changes, they focus on some of the more microlevel endings: the end of the book, literature, and theory—and our responses to them.

All three—books, literature, and theory—are going through a period now where many see their best days as behind them. The essays here take up these topics, not with a nostalgic nod to the past or utopian utterances to the future but rather firmly situated in the present—a period that expanded out becomes the contemporary and contracted back reduces to the daily. "Every word," says Ralph Berry of this essay style, "is written in the present, and where the present's meaning is staked, nothing will substitute for belief."

But the late age of print has its beginnings too. The most important of which might be the self-publishing revolution—one that also impacts books, literature, and theory. With this revolution comes the freedom to self-publish heterodox literature as well as theory without the usual gatekeeping apparatus of the publishing industry. And while mainstream publishing may not have the will to support work critical of the dark paths taken by capitalism, democracy, and America today, the self-publishing revolution means that this is no longer a cause for concern. The title of this book, *The End of American Literature*, is meant to evoke the dynamics and stakes of the late age of print as well as signal the changing role of books, literature, and theory in American life. It also signals that the changes may be more than ones of media modality, but also ones that affect the very literature we consider American.

1

Saints and Critics

Printers and brewers share a saint.

Augustine of Hippo serves as the patron saint of brewers in recognition of the raucous life he lived prior to his conversion to Christianity and the patron saint of printers for his extensive writings on his faith.

He is also the patron saint of theologians, and is regarded by many historians of philosophy as the most influential philosopher in Western history.

Before his conversion, he was a teacher of rhetoric. He is also widely credited for developing the first "hermeneutics" in his book, *On Christian Doctrine* (397/426 C.E.).

Augustine of Hippo, or St. Augustine, if you will, is as at home in religious circles as he is in literary and philosophical. He practiced poverty and charity, and made enormous contributions to Western philosophical thought.

He is one those writers we love to hate.

The confluence of devotion and depravity, the secular and the spiritual, and the pious and impure makes him one of the more difficult figures in the Western canon.

With Augustine, we always already bring a Catholic Saint and Church Father into our "secular" classrooms. Emphasizing his Berber and North African descent by calling him Augustine "of Hippo" does nothing to divorce him from his founding influence on early Christianity. In the twenty-first century, to bring this "saint" into our classrooms is to risk religious "advocacy," particularly if unaccompanied by representation from other faiths.

Still, I cannot imagine literature or literary theory without him.

Compared to Augustine, our love/hate relationships with contemporary writers seem trivial, even when measured against the extremes.

Barring the much-debated and well-documented controversies over the alleged Nazi ties of Martin Heidegger and Paul de Man, two of the patron saints of deconstruction, another, less considered controversy is maybe more relevant to considerations of critical sainthood and moral opprobrium: the case of Christopher Hitchens' attacks on Mother Teresa.

Hitchens began as a journalist with the *New Statesman* in Britain. Over the course of his career, he contributed mountains of cultural criticism for many different publications including *The Nation*, *The Atlantic*, *Slate*, *Harper's*, *The New York Times Book Review*, and *Vanity Fair*, as well as many other publications both in America and abroad.

Widely regarded on the lecture circuit, he seemed willing to debate anyone on anything. His firebrand-style of criticism made him one of the most recognized (and loathed) public intellectuals in the world by the time of his death in 2011. Though Hitchens was a darling of the left, he was independent enough in his thinking to break ranks with it, for example to support the invasion of Iraq.

Perhaps his most notorious and iconoclastic body of criticism came in response to the charitable work of Mother Teresa. In 1992, he wrote a column critical of her work in *The Nation* entitled "Mother Teresa: Ghoul of Calcutta." The following year, in an interview on C-SPAN, he said of the negative response to his criticisms of her, "If you touch the idea of sainthood, especially in this country, people feel you've taken something from them personally. I'm fascinated because we like to look down on other religious beliefs as being tribal and superstitious but never dare criticize our own."

Then, in 1994, Hitchens and British Pakistani journalist Tariq Ali wrote a documentary called "Hell's Angel: Mother Teresa of Calcutta." It was shown in November of the same year on British television on Channel Four's arts series "Without Walls." Their work drew heavily from the account of Aroup Chatterjee, an Indian-born British writer who had worked in one of Teresa's charitable homes. Hitchens then followed up "Hell's Angel" with a pamphlet published by Verso in 1995 entitled *The Missionary Position: Mother Teresa in Theory and Practice.*

In his review of the book in *The New York Times*, Bruno Maddox says that Hitchens' conclusion is that Mother Teresa was "less interested in helping the poor than in using them as an indefatigable source of wretchedness on which to fuel the expansion of her fundamentalist Roman Catholic beliefs."

Years later, when the Archdiocese of Washington was considering Mother Teresa for sainthood in 2001, Hitchens testified against it saying she "was not a friend of the poor" but rather a "friend of poverty" and "the worst of the rich."

These and other attacks on Mother Teresa polarized opinion about Hitchens. Many came to hate him and still do. Others saw him as speaking "truth" to the "power" of the Catholic Church, and found his commentary on Teresa and the Church to be critically heroic.

But even many of those who agree with his criticisms of Teresa call him a "troublemaker." Taking on an internationally beloved person who received the Nobel Prize for Peace for her work with the poor of India is not the definition of a "peacemaker." Doing it repeatedly over an international chorus of opposition is the very definition of "troublemaking."

In spite of Hitchens' efforts, Mother Teresa became a saint a few years ago. For many, her name remains synonymous with human goodness and moral saintliness, and his associated with the opposite.

But for those who champion critics and criticism, it is hard not to find in the example of Hitchens' body of work the kind of commentary worthy of critical sainthood.

To be sure, in spite of her legion of admirers, over the years many others have questioned her charitable work and the nature of her legacy though none as controversially as Hitchens.

For example, in India, the site of most of her charitable work, she was roundly criticized by the head of the Hindu nationalist group Rashtriya Swayamsevak Sangh.

"It's good to work for a cause with selfless intentions," said Mohan Bhagwat, chief of Rashtriya Swayamsevak Sangh, at the opening of an orphanage in India in 2014, a year before her canonization.

"But Mother Teresa's work had [an] ulterior motive, which was to convert the person who was being served to Christianity." "In the name of service, religious conversions were made. This was followed by other institutes, too."

Bhagwat reignited a firestorm by following Hitchens in questioning the intentions of Mother Teresa.

One Congress Party official, Rajiv Shukla, demanded an apology from Bhagwat, and the chief minister of Delhi, Arvind Kejriwal, asked the Rashtriya Swayamsevak Sangh to spare this "noble soul" from criticism.

But what does it really mean to "spare" someone from criticism? Particularly someone who has been the subject of international scrutiny dating back over two decades, that is, to at least Hitchens' 1992 article in *The Nation*? Is this even possible today?

To "spare" someone or something criticism is to give them or it a pass at a time in history where nothing is above criticism or sacrosanct—not even saints. A case might be made though that critics like Hitchens were only possible in the late age of print; only possible in a time where media gatekeepers could still regulate the flow of commentary through controlling access to print, radio, and television.

Hitchens was the kind of media spectacle that sold magazines and brought viewers to television—and was well paid to do it. But the dawn of the digital age changed the media and critical landscape. No one is immune from criticism in the digital age and everyone is free to contribute it. As long as the commentary generates traffic or gets hits or clicks it does not matter the source of it or even the veracity.

But before we criticize Hitchens for being a tool of the late print-age media machine, a critic that everyone "loved to hate" for his strong, controversial, and witty opinions, remember his other major media foray was in defense of free speech and artistic freedom.

In 1988, Salman Rushdie published a novel entitled *The Satanic Verses.* Though Rushdie and Hitchens had been friends since the mid-1980s, they did not become close friends until Ayatollah Khomeini of Iran called for the death of Rushdie and everyone "involved in its publication" on Valentine's Day 1989. According to Rushdie, writing in *Vanity Fair* just after Hitchens's death, Khomeini's religious edict "changed something in Christopher." "It made him understand that a new danger had been unleashed upon the earth, that a new totalizing ideology had stepped into the down-at-the-heels shoes of Soviet Communism."

As a result of Khomeini's *fatwa*, a short time later, writes Hitchens in his reflections on the event twenty years later in Vanity Fair, aptly entitled, "Assassins of the Mind": "Hitoshi Igarashi, the Japanese translator of *The Satanic Verses,* was stabbed to death on the campus where he taught literature, and the Italian translator Ettore Capriolo was knifed in his apartment in Milan. William Nygaard, the novel's Norwegian publisher, was shot three times in the back and left for dead outside his Oslo home." As for Rushdie himself, there were several attempts on his life but none were successful.

"And all this," writes Hitchens, "because the senile Khomeini, who had publicly promised that he would never make a deal with Saddam Hussein because god was on the Iranian side, had had to swallow the poison (as he put it) of signing a treaty after all, and was urgently in need of a crowd-pleasing 'issue' that would restore his purist religious credentials."

Hitchens called the *fatwa* "the single worst review any novelist has ever had"—and it is hard even today to disagree with him.

While some came to the defense of Rushdie, many more did not, including President H. W. Bush, who had no comment because, in the words of Hitchens, "no American interest was involved." "I doubt he would have said this," continues Hitchens, "if the chairman of Texaco had been hit with a *fatwa*." For him, the United States *did* have an interest, namely, "an interest in opposing state-sponsored terrorism against novelists."

"Various intellectualoids, from John Berger on the left to Norman Podhoretz on the right, argued that Rushdie got what he deserved for insulting a great religion," writes Hitchens in his 2009 article "Assassins of the Mind." So too did "the Tory historian Hugh Trevor-Roper, and the doyen of espionage authors John Le Carré, [who] also pronounced that Rushdie was the author of his own troubles, and had brought them on himself by 'offending' a great monotheistic religion," wrote Hitchens in his book *God Is Not Great: How Religion Poisons Everything* (2007).

In his 2010 memoir, *Hitch-22*, Hitchens recalls being asked for a comment on the *fatwa* a few hours after it was announced by Khomeini: "I felt at once that here was something that completely committed me. It was, if I can phrase it like this, a matter of everything I hated versus everything I loved. In the hate column: dictatorship, religion, stupidity, demagogy, censorship, bullying, and intimidation. In the love column: literature, irony, humor, the individual, and the defense of free expression."

Hitchens thought both in 1989 as well in 2009 that the Rushdie *fatwa* "was not just a warning of what was to come." "It was *the* warning." He was fighting a battle against "dictatorship, religion, stupidity, demagogy, censorship, bullying, and intimidation"—a battle that rages on today with even greater intensity.

And, believe it or not, so too does the Rushdie *fatwa*.

Apparently, a religious fatwa is not reversible. "Nobody in the world can nullify a religious fatwa," said a senior member of the editorial team at the state-run Fars News Agency in Tehran. "It has been, it is, and it will be."

While it can't be nullified, a bounty can be added to it. In 2016 it was widely reported that "over 40 state-run media outlets in Iran have raised $600,000 to add as bounty to Ayatollah Khomeini's death fatwa on the writer Salman Rushdie."

While Hitchens is no longer around to defend his friends against acts of terrorism against novelists, many others are stepping up in defense of free expression. But are they enough? Who among us invests as much energy as Hitchens did in the war against dictatorships, religion, stupidity, demagogy, censorship, bullying, and intimidation?

"I have often been asked if Christopher defended me because he was my close friend," said Rushdie. "The truth is that he became my close friend because he wanted to defend me."

Writers we love to hate come in different forms: some are saints like Augustine and others are sinners like Hitchens. But if Augustine was a sinner before he became a saint, why not Hitchens? Critics could use a patron saint, too.

2

Therapy for the Novel

The Western Regional Psychoanalytic Association of America was impressed.

While many were awaiting the end of the world—or at least a big computer crash—they were opening the new millennium by presenting two of the writers of *The Sopranos* television series an award for their depiction of Tony Soprano's therapy sessions.

Not the end of the world, but a big step for psychoanalysts.

The following year Lorraine Bracco, who plays Dr. Jennifer Melfi in the series—mobster Soprano's therapist—was also given an award by the association.

When asked about it, Bracco reportedly said, "What, are they crazy? I'm *so* not Dr. Melfi."

While the association could probably have devoted an entire conference to just Bracco's response to her award, they were otherwise occupied basking in the glow brought to their profession by television.

The Sopranos, a television series by David Chase that ran from 1999 to 2007, gave psychoanalytic theory a popular shot in the arm. Not only was the general public tuning in at record numbers each week to see what "America's favorite family" was up to but so too were psychologists and psychiatrists. By the end of the third season in 2001, *The Sopranos* had become "must-see TV for psychologists and psychiatrists, especially the psychoanalytically inclined," writes Lawrence R. Samuel in *Shrink: A Cultural History of Psychoanalysis in America* (2013). Viewership for the final episode of the series was estimated to be almost 12 million viewers.

"It's the best representation of the work we do," said Philip Ringstrom, an analyst at the Institute of Contemporary Psychoanalysis in Los Angeles, "that ever has been in film or on television."

Praise like this from professional analysts for the depiction of the therapeutic experience on *The Sopranos* was coupled with even higher praise for the public relations work the series was doing for psychoanalysis in the new millennium. Ringstrom and others would regularly comment after episodes on *Slate*—and even the American Psychological Association tacitly acknowledged the impact of the series, scheduling Ringstrom to give a presentation to a packed house on the therapeutic aspects of *The Sopranos*.

But the excitement about *The Sopranos* was not limited to just psychologists. Novelists from Norman Mailer to Gary Shteyngart have described this television series as a Great American Novel. And literary critics have compared Chase to Charles Dickens.

Seeking to cash in on the success of the series, the *New York Times* even asked Michael Chabon, Elmore Leonard, and Michael Connelly to revive in its *Magazine*, the serial novel—the closest narrative equivalent to eight years and 86 episodes of televised mob life.

The close of the series though did not end the conversation about the potential of serialized television for American novelistic greatness.

In the midst one of the worst economic collapses in American history, another great work of serial television was born.

Breaking Bad aired its first episode on January 20, 2008. Its protagonist, Walter White (played by Bryan Cranston), was a former graduate student and high school teacher who turned to cooking and dealing meth to secure a solid financial future for his family. If the unconscious of Tony Soprano and its role in the sociopathic violence in which he participates is the driving force of *The Sopranos*, then the post-Freudian schizophrenic neoliberal unconsciousness is the driving machine of *Breaking Bad*. Gilles Deleuze and Felix Guattari are to *Breaking Bad* what Sigmund Freud and Jacques Lacan are to *The Sopranos*.

From 2008 to 2013, *Breaking Bad* had us following the raging schizophrenic lives of Walter White and Heisenberg, his alter ego, as they voyaged deeper and deeper into the neoliberal abyss of America. His journey from indebted man to meth entrepreneur to death only furthered the case that a Great American Novel may be before you, but not on the shelf of a bookstore.

Similar cases might be made too for *The Wire*, which ran from 2002 to 2008; *Mad Men*, which ran from 2007 to 2015; or even *House of Cards*, which began in 2013 but is now in production chaos because of one of its lead character's alleged history of sexual harassment. In fact, David Simon, creator of *The Wire*, pitched the series to the network as a "60-hour long 'visual novel.'" An exciting pitch for fans of, say, graphic fiction but still pale in comparison to the one *Mad Men*'s Don Draper did for Hershey Bars.

The list of serial television productions post-*Sopranos* has of course multiplied. Twelve million viewers gets the attention of corporate media executives who have been—in spite of the blip with *House of Cards*—churning out one new televised "serial" or "visual" novel after another.

Historical hindsight will help separate the genre's Homer from its has-beens; its Dickenses and Dostoevskyes from its duds. But to keep it out of the conversation of American literary greatness is to forget from whence not just American literature came but literature in general. These long-form series are not only one of the more notable developments of the Golden Age of television they are also one of the more amazing developments of literature in the age of new media.

But in the process they have reversed the traditional relationship of new media to literature. Instead of PBS bringing the classics to the small screen, television is creating classics on it. For some the "greatness appeal" of some contemporary television is a problem for the novel. Who, they ask, is going to step up and make the novel "great again" at a time when television is attracting increasing viewership and aspiring in its own writing to levels of excellence that rival those of the novel? But I'm not one of those people.

So what if it is now the film or the television series that needs to be turned into the novel, rather than the other way around? And so what if this never happens—after all, how many films ever reached the greatness of their novels? Why repeat the cycle and ask it now of the great television series?

John Freeman, a former president of the National Book Critics Circle, took up the question of whether *The Sopranos* "murdered" the novel. His response reminds us of both the parallels between the series and the novel, and its differences.

"*The Sopranos*," writes Freeman, "covered some of the primary themes of the Great American Novel." "Like Jonathan Franzen's *The Corrections*," he continues, "it explored the ways in which each new generation attempts to fix the parenting mistakes of the one before; like John Updike's *Rabbit* tetralogy, it hitched its star to the emotionally complicated but intellectually unsophisticated inner life of an unreconstructed American man; and like Philip Roth's *American Pastoral*, it depicted the death of an American city, revealing the rupture between classes (and races) around its grave." But for all of its thematic similarity, the value of reading novels for Freeman is fundamentally different than the value of viewing television. And given that the series facilitates the latter but not the former, it needs to be regarded more in line with the death of reading—and by extension, the novel—than with new forms or high expressions of it.

Unlike Freeman, I'm more inclined to take the long view on *The Sopranos*—and its kindred series. I see in the best of them a deep theoretical examination of some of the problems facing our world today in a way that appeals to a popular audience. Some of these shows can even contribute to theoretical investigations often merely relegated only to scholarly or professional audiences. That a television show could reawaken interest in psychoanalysis, a theory left for dead by many in the dustbin of the new millennium, is a good thing for theory *and* literature.

Freeman too moves in this direction but ultimately does not embrace it.

"In a funk," says Freeman, "Tony turns to psychotherapy to repair the psychic breach created for him by living beyond his background, only to carom out." "Freud's narratives," continues Freeman, "mean nothing to him when compared to those of Francis Ford Coppola." Nevertheless, in spite of the timeless allure of lines like *The Godfather*'s (1972) "Leave the gun, take the cannoli," Tony continues with his therapy throughout the series. In other words, he continues to give theory a chance in spite of the many distractions and other influences in his life.

And if our mobster prefers the films of Francis Ford Coppola to Freudian theory, this only makes him more like us—as so too do many *theorists* today. It is not that Freud does not speak to us about our world, it is that Coppola's Corleone gang is *our gang*—their world feels more like our world than the world of the Viennese father of psychoanalysis.

The Sopranos is not the death of the novel. Nor is television or film. It is about the rebirth of psychoanalytic theory in an unexpected place like serial television.

As those who have watched *The Sopranos* know, Tony has a complicated relationship with both his therapist and therapy. Psychoanalysis too as a theory and practice has gone through its own ups and downs ever since Freud's day. Not only are there many different rifts and schools within psychoanalytic theory, the practice itself has long been the subject of not just critical scrutiny, but also literary derision. Just consider Henry Miller's famous passage on it from his 1949 novel, *Sexus:*

> Lie down, then, on the soft couch which the analyst provides, and try to think up something different. The analyst has endless time and patience; every minute you detain him means money in his pocket. He is like God, in a sense—the God of your own creation. Whether you whine, howl, beg, weep, implore, pray or curse—he listens. He is just a big ear minus a sympathetic nervous system. He is impervious to everything but truth. If you think it pays to fool him then fool him. Who will be the loser? If you think he can help you, and not yourself, then stick to him until you rot. He has nothing to lose.

Literary derision of therapy like Miller's only makes the popular success of it in *The Sopranos* all the more impressive. But just for a moment, imagine the series without Dr. Melfi treating Tony Soprano. What if Tony rejected the couch and the cost of the analyst? What if he rejected psychoanalytic theory? What then is the alternative?

Without the unconscious of Tony Soprano on display to account for the violence in his world, the series would descend into merely yet one more glorification of it. But short of this, there is another plot twist possible for the series should Tony decide to reject therapy. Again, it comes from Miller:

> But if you realize he is not a god but a human being like yourself, with worries, defects, ambitions, frailties, that he is not the repository of an all-encompassing wisdom but a wanderer, like yourself, along the path, perhaps you will cease pouring it out like a sewer, however melodious it may sound to your ears, and rise up on your own two legs and sing with your own God-given voice. To confess, to whine, to complain, to commiserate, always demands a toll. To sing it doesn't cost you a penny. Not only does it cost nothing—you actually enrich others. *Sing the praises of the Lord*, it is enjoined. Aye, sing out! Sing out, O Master-builder! Sing out, glad warrior!

Miller's response to rejecting psychoanalysis here is both surprising and poetically empowering. Who would have imagined Tony singing songs as replacements for the scenes with Dr. Melfi? But this call to song might also be taken as a call to storytelling, which is precisely what *The Sopranos* does—tells a story.

Not only are there echoes of Walt Whitman's poetic calls for song in Miller but so too are there Homer's:

> Rage—Goddess, sing the rage of Peleus' son Achilles,
> Murderous, doomed, that cost the Acheans countless losses,
> Hurling down the House of Death so many sturdy souls,
> great fighters' souls, but made their bodies carrion,
> feasts for the dogs and birds,
> and the will of Zeus was moving toward its end.

But if singing of the rage of Tony Soprano and all of the sturdy mobsters who died off during the course of 86 episodes of Chase's *The Sopranos* feels small next to the quarrel between Achilles and Agamemnon in Homer's *The Illiad*, this is only an historical contingency.

Those who gathered around to hear songs of Achilles in preliterate Greece form a narrative line with those who gather around the television to watch Tony Soprano lie on the couch for Dr. Melfi. The gaps over the millennia are filled with scores of narrative forms "staged," in the words of literary critic Alan Singer, "within the framework of social-temporal conditions."

Miller helps us to imagine a place for *The Sopranos* without psychoanalysis. But as the song he suggests echoes the song of Homer, we come full circle back to the series itself as a kind of narrative of epic dimensions. Or, in more contemporary terms, as a kind of Great American novel. And why not?

The genealogy of the novel has been continuously contested and debated. For some, the form points back to the oral traditions of the ancient world. For others, the novel emerging in the epistolary forms of the eighteenth century, heightening in the serial forms of late nineteenth-century print capitalism, and culminated in doorstop fictions like Don De Lillo's *Underworld* (1997)—or even controversial earlier works like Miller's *Rosy Crucifixion* trilogy, *Sexus*, 1949; *Plexus*, 1953; and *Nexus*, 1959—which were banned in the U.S. until 1964.

With so much disagreement over what the novel is and is not, adding "visual novels" to the list of its possible forms is not a stretch, especially in the age of new media.

Like the Western Regional Psychoanalytic Association of America, we too should award the writers of *The Sopranos*. Their television series as well as those that have followed in its footsteps are not only challenging the boundaries of the novel, they are also contributing to critical insight into our broken world. Whether this insight comes through singing, reading, or viewing is less important than calling on our own Muses in response to dark times.

Miller too warns us about splitting hairs over form while those who are offering resistance in dark times are being persecuted:

"*But*, you quibble, how can I sing when the world is crumbling, when all about me is bathed in blood and tears? Do you realize that the martyrs sang when they were being burned at the stake?"

Thinking about psychoanalytic theory in *The Sopranos* reminds us about the therapy our own world needs today. Maybe too it provides a kind of therapy for the novel. But while I would like to know as much as anyone in the field of contemporary American literature the source of the next Great American Novel, worry about our nation's reckless push to *American greatness* occupies more of my current critical interest.

Television can provide insight into both theory and its toolbox for critical resistance. Whether it is critical insight into a narcissistic mob leader like Tony Soprano or Walter White, the exemplary neoliberal man, our toolbox for critical resistance can grow with each episode. The question remains though whether its songs or others will be the ones sung by those who will unjustly burn for raging against the sources of our crumbling world.

Only time will tell.

3

Slow Philosophy

Slow and low? Or fast and loud? Led Zeppelin or Metallica? Hydraulics or Hemis?

When it comes to rock music and custom cars, opinions are sharply divided. Does the same hold for reading and writing? Speech and argument? Is loud argument preferable to low? Fast reading to slow?

While the "need for speed" is more than adequately represented in our culture, the "slow movement" has been catching on ever since the publication of Carl Honoré's *In Praise of Slowness: Challenging the Cult of Speed* in 2004.

"These days," writes Honoré, "we exist to serve the economy, rather than the other way around." As servants of what he calls "turbo-capitalism," we pay a heavy cost.

"Long hours on the job are making us unproductive, error-prone, unhappy and ill," says Honoré. "Doctor's offices are swamped with people suffering from conditions brought on by stress: insomnia, migraines, hypertension, asthma and gastrointestinal trouble, to name but a few." And while a vacation would lessen the suffering, on average Americans only use eighty percent of their paid time off, while only forty percent of workers in the U.K. use their full vacation entitlement.

The work of Honoré, a Canadian journalist based in London, has led to a spate of "slow" books and articles. There is the slow food movement, the Slow Science Academy, and various slow "philosophy" manifestos. The Australian magazine simply entitled *Slow* is dedicated to "promoting the slow philosophy." Michelle Boulous Walker's *Slow Philosophy: Reading against the Institution* (2017), argues that philosophy teaches us to read slowly, something which "inevitably clashes with many of our current institutional practices and demands."

Another recent book, *The Slow Professor: Challenging the Culture of Speed in the Academy* (2016), contends that academics must slow down. Authors Maggie Berg and Barbara K. Seeber argue that "adopting the principles of Slow in our professional practice is an effective way to alleviate work stress, preserve humanistic education, and resist the corporate university." Who would have contended that *napping* has the potential to bring down neoliberal academe?

To be sure, in the age of the internet and social media, speed is the key. Faster, shorter, and often shriller messages are seen as most effective. Concentration has given way to skimming; attention to inattention; and depth to surface. This manifests itself in a public discourse that favors the fast and loud over the slow and low. In politics and public life, more focus is given to those who yell. Those who take time to think before they speak are at a disadvantage.

Pundits scream at each other at a rapid-fire pace about anything and everything in the hopes of gaining greater attention for themselves and their sponsors. Dialogue and debate degenerates in this climate into demagoguery and diatribe. The content of the speech of the pundit is secondary to its performative aspects. Hyperbole gets social media attention and more hits on the internet than measured opinion, which is often relegated to noncommercial venues like PBS.

Writers and thinkers need to consider our own practices and preferences. We aim for fast book sales over slow sales. We champion the book that flies off the shelf over the novel that takes years to gain an audience. We admire the relentlessly self-promoting author, busy with readings and other promotional activities. We look for bold and hyperbolic praise in our reviews, preferring a quick thumbs up or five-star promotion over a subtle analysis weighing merits and contextualizing a work in literary and intellectual traditions.

In a driven environment intensified by the insatiable financial appetites of corporate America, calm, careful, unhurried, patient, and reflective commentary about writing and writers does not increase the bottom line of the neoliberal publishing industry as effectively as aggressive, inattentive, hurried, and superficial commentary. The loud voices muffle out the low ones in the book world. And they are indeed fast and furious in the age of digital communication.

To take the other road in American publishing—the one where the voices are not so loud and the pace not as fast—is to take the road of small and independent press publishing. Its philosophical roots are not with the free-market economics of Milton Friedman, but rather with another albeit unlikely source: the philologically inspired "slow and low" philosophy of the nineteenth-century German philosopher Friedrich Nietzsche.

"But, after all," wrote Nietzsche, "why must we proclaim so loudly and with such intensity what we are, what we want, and what we do not want?" "Let us look at this more calmly and wisely; for a higher and more distant point of view," he continued. "Let us proclaim it, as if among ourselves, in so low a tone that all the world fails to hear it and *us*!"

Nietzsche is encouraging us here to take the long view on things. There is no need to shout out to the world what we are, what we want, and what we do not want, but rather to be content to whisper it in a voice so low that we are not heard. The context for these remarks is a preface he wrote some years later to his 1881 book *Morgenröthe*, which is alternately translated as *The Dawn of the Day* or simply *Daybreak*.

It is somewhat ironic to point out that Nietzsche saw *Daybreak* as the start of a "campaign" of sorts of his own, writing in one of his final books, *Ecce Homo* (1888), "With the book [*Daybreak*], I open my campaign against morality." Of course, a "campaign against morality" is something that is difficult to keep quiet, especially since his work takes as its target much of the history of morality in Western philosophy. It is almost as if he is suggesting that the louder the subject the lower the voice we should use to announce it. But of course he is not.

Much of the writing published by small presses in America follows Nietzsche's line of thinking here though maybe not out of choice but of financial necessity. The literature of the small presses of America is also the literature of the small markets of America. It does not attract a large readership and it does not spin the large wheels of the market. Through the eyes of the neoliberal publishing industry, because of its low sales and readership, it is a failure. However, through the eyes of Nietzsche, we have another way to view it. Namely, a way that questions the necessity of loudly proclaiming its presence to the world, and offers to us the suggestion that we should be more than satisfied to proclaim it just among ourselves. Against the grain of the literary pundits shouting out the virtues of their preferred writers and writings as the fuel for market saturation of the literary commodity, Nietzsche encourages the small presses of the world to promote their publications "in so low a tone that all the world fails to hear it" and *them*! And with this low tone, take the low and slow road to successful thought and writing.

But Nietzsche here is not just advocating that we turn down the volume, he is also encouraging us to slow things down too, particularly when it comes to our writing. Though much of his own work went to press very soon after its composition, he spent much of his writing life revising his books for new editions and posterity. In the case of *Daybreak*, though first published in 1881, it was not until five years later that he wrote the wonderful preface to it that we are now considering.

"This preface comes late," wrote Nietzsche, "but not too late; what, after all, do five or six years matter?" Can you imagine a writer saying something like this to a corporate publisher today?

I remember some years back when I was working on my own ethics book, telling my editor that it was going to take more time for me to complete the project than I had initially projected. Though it was not five or six years, it was a significant chunk of additional time that I needed. Lack of experience with corporate publishing (and probably too much Nietzsche) led me to think that this was no big deal. Well, boy was *I* wrong.

The editor's face turned bright red and he literally started foaming at the mouth as he proceeded to yell at me about the financial significance of deadlines and the perils of trying to turn a book on morality into an "Irish novel." Though I did not know this passage from Nietzsche at the time, in retrospect, I don't think it would have helped to deescalate the situation. Corporate publishing waits for no one—not even philosophy!

"Such a book, such a problem, are in no hurry; besides, we are friends of the *lento*, I and my book," writes Nietzsche of the book that started his campaign against morality. And he continues:

> I have not been a philologist in vain—perhaps I am one yet: a teacher of slow reading. I even come to write slowly. At present it is not only my habit, but even my taste—a perverted taste, maybe—to write nothing but what will drive to despair every one who is "in a hurry."

The low volumes now become slow paces. The philologist takes in words slowly and is slow to produce them because he does not take them lightly. This "slow philosophy" of Nietzsche is maddening to all those want to amplify the volume of literature, and rush the pace of writing and reading. The nod back to philology by Nietzsche is a smack in the face of speed writing and speed reading—and the genres and institutions that enable it.

For philology is that venerable art which exacts from its followers one thing above all—to step to one side, to leave themselves spare moments, to grow silent, to become slow—the leisurely art of the goldsmith applied to language: an art which must carry out slow, fine work, and attains nothing if not *lento.* For this very reason philology is now more desirable than ever before; for this very reason it is the highest attraction and incitement in an age of "work": that is to say, of haste, of unseemly and immoderate hurry-skurry, which is intent upon "getting things done" at once, even every book, whether old or new. Philology itself, perhaps, will not "get things done" so hurriedly: it teaches how to read *well: i.e.* slowly, profoundly, attentively, prudently, with inner thoughts, with mental doors ajar, with delicate fingers and eyes.

While I will break with Nietzsche regarding advocacy for a return to philology today, I will side with him when it comes to his recommendation that we learn how to read slowly. This is the preferred method of the critic. Fittingly, it is also the way of the philosopher.

To read "slowly, profoundly, attentively, prudently, with inner thoughts, with mental doors ajar, with delicate fingers and eyes" is to reject the pundits who yell at the top of their voices anything that comes to their mind. It is also to look to the kinds of writing that lend themselves to slow reading and slow writing. And, following Nietzsche, to slow re-reading and re-*writing.*

Nietzsche knew his own work required a very special kind of reader. It is not the sort of thing one picks up to turn pages quickly. It is dense, aphoristic writing that requires patience and time. He went so far as to say in his 1886 preface to the book that *Daybreak* "appeals only to perfect readers and philologists," asking this very select audience to exercise the patience to "*learn* to read me well!"

Today not all great philosophers are slow writers. Jean-Paul Sartre and Slavoj Žižek have disabused us of this. But most philosophy worth reading still requires a level of attentiveness contrary to the speed of life in the new millennium.

Today, "philosophy in a minute" is widely preferred to plowing through the long and dense writings of the Nietzsche's of the world. The "flash philosophy" of the dictionary, Wikipedia entry, handbook, and compendium is the philosophical analogue to one of the newer genres of writing, "flash fiction." In a world aimed at increasing speed rather than decreasing it, philosophy and literature are out of place except as bite-size snacks.

So, fast philosophy or slow philosophy? Perhaps knowing that the pace of philosophy is ill-suited to the ends of the neoliberal economy and its spawn, corporate publishing and the neoliberal university, will help you decide to join with Nietzsche and the "friends of the *lento*."

Slow is the speed of philosophy—and low its tone.

4

Publishing Genius

"I am a genius in a nice, small way."
—Horace Liveright to Lucille Liveright, January 13, 1922

The history of film is filled with many memorable films about writers—both real and imagined.

On the imaginary side, there is *As Good As It Gets* (1997), *Barton Fink* (1991), *Breakfast at Tiffany's* (1961), *Deconstructing Harry* (1997), *Fear and Loathing in Las Vegas* (1998), *Finding Forester* (2000), *Heartburn* (1986), *Love and Death on Long Island* (1997), *My Left Foot* (1989), *The Third Man* (1949), and *Wonder Boys* (2000).

On the real side, there is *The Adventures of Mark Twain* (1944), *Balzac: A Life of Passion* (1999), *Henry and June* (1990, on Henry Miller), *Jack London* (1943), *Kafka* (1991), *The Life of Emile Zola* (1937), *The Passion of Ayn Rand* (1999), *Shadowlands* (1993, on C. S. Lewis), *Shakespeare in Love* (1998), *Tom and Viv* (1994, on T. S. Eliot), *Oscar Wilde* (1960), and *Wilde* (1997).

We could spill a lot of ink debating how realistic are the imaginary writers and how imaginary are the real writers in these films.

We could also carry on quite a bit about "Top 10" films about writers and writing as there are literally hundreds of films in this category.

But when we move from one side of the publishing fence to the other, that is, from writers to publishers and editors, the list of films is much shorter—and far less memorable. How many films can you recall about editors or publishers? Let alone films with strong claims to cinematic greatness like *Shakespeare in Love* or *The Third Man*?

The earliest film about a book publisher was *The Scoundrel* released on April 30, 1935.

That year, Franklin D. Roosevelt was halfway through his first of four terms as president and the best-selling book was *Green Light* by Lloyd C. Douglas.

Co-directed and co-written by Ben Hecht and Charles MacArthur, *The Scoundrel* was inspired, in part, by the life of the famed publisher Horace Liveright, who had died two years earlier.

Liveright, the publisher of T. S. Eliot's *The Waste Land* (1922) and Theodore Dreiser's *An American Tragedy* (1925) as well as first books by Ernest Hemingway, William Faulkner, Hart Crane, and Dorothy Parker, co-founded Boni & Liveright in 1917. He also founded an inexpensive reprint line called "Modern Library" the same year.

Five years later, based on the flip of a coin (according to Bennett Cerf), Liveright bought out his partner Albert Boni, after their relationship broke down. Two years later, in 1925, he then infamously sold Modern Library to his vice-president, Bennett Cerf, because of personal financial difficulties.

In 1924, Liveright became stage-struck and started to produce plays, including *Dracula*, which featured Bela Lugosi in the lead role. But the plays and lavish parties he was known to hold took their financial toll on him and, in 1928, he lost control of Boni & Liveright and, by 1930, was out of the publishing company entirely. Years of alcoholism then took its physical toll on him and he died of pneumonia three years later, penniless, at the age of forty-nine.

The rise and fall of Liveright is a legendary story in the publishing world. Whereas in July of 1928 his company was publisher of six of the top ten best-selling books in America, five years later he was broke and dead, with only a handful of people attending his funeral.

A letter dated September 27, 1933, to Una Jeffers, wife of Robinson Jeffers, by Cerf, who attended the funeral, sums up well the rise and fall of Liveright:

> What a tragic end it was for this man whose star was so high in the heavens only a few short years ago! He died penniless and utterly broken in spirit, and even authors who owed their whole start in life to him didn't have the grace to turn up at the last services. Upton Sinclair spoke a few words, and very badly too, I thought. The only newspaperman present was Harry Hansen, the reviewer for the Evening Telegram. As Hansen put it, Liveright had no more advertising appropriations to hand out.

In *The Scoundrel*, the publisher in the film is a character named Anthony Mallare, who is played by Noël Coward in his cinematic "debut" (he previously had a bit part in a silent film). Mallare is a publisher who seems dead set on destroying everyone with whom he comes into contact, and Coward does a great job living up to the film's title. In the film, Mallare works with a young author (Ridges), and manages to destroy both his career and his life. When Ridges's girlfriend hears that Mallare has died in a plane crash in the ocean, she exclaims, "I've just found out there *is* a God!"

Though the film won an Academy Award for Best Original Story for its writers, Hecht and MacArthur, it is as unflattering a portrayal of a publisher as one can imagine.

It is also probably the first and last portrayal of a publisher in the history of Hollywood film. I do not know of any other films centered around the life—real or imaginary—of a book publisher. But it does not mean that *The Scoundrel* was not an influential film.

In *Book Business* (2001), Jason Epstein, the celebrated executive editor of Random House, recalls that he decided on a career in publishing after watching the film. In 1950, he interviewed for a position at Doubleday. "I knew nothing about book publishing," writes Epstein, "beyond what I learned the week before I joined Doubleday from a film called *The Scoundrel*." It "convinced me to take the job at Doubleday that I had been offered the week before."

But Epstein also says that he learned later that Liveright "had not been a scoundrel at all." One of the screenwriters, Hecht, had worked for Liveright and "hated him." "He was a brilliantly innovative if suicidal publisher addicted to drink and dangerous love affairs," comments Epstein of Liveright. "He was as handsome as Coward himself, with an uncanny eye for talent and the promotional instincts of Barnum at a time when writers of genius were turning up on both sides of the Atlantic but were generally shunned by the genteel publishers of the day."

Epstein even goes so far as to claim, "If not for Joyce's anti-Semitic American advisor, who refused to cooperate, Liveright would have fought the censors over *Ulysses* a decade before Random House took the case to court and won." In other words, *Ulysses*, the book that launched Random House, could have very easily have been published by Boni & Liveright. On January 4, 1922, Liveright had dinner with Pound, Eliot, and Joyce. By the end of dinner that night, he had retained the services of Pound as his European "book scout" for

$500 a year, and had agreed to publish *The Waste Land* for a $150 advance and the unexpurgated text of Ulysses for a $1,000 advance.

In addition to Eliot, Hemingway, Dreiser, Crane, Parker, and Faulkner, Liveright also published works by Eugene O'Neill, E. E. Cummings, Djuna Barnes, S. J. Perelman, Peter Arno, Nathanael West, and Sigmund Freud. Among this baker's dozen of writers is an ample representation of writing genius from the latter part of the nineteenth century and early part of the twentieth. Though Liveright did not discover all of these writers (for example, he signed Dreiser at a 25 percent royalty fairly late in his career, and offered to reissue all of his earlier titles, a deal which turned out in the long run to be a mistake) or even read them all (for example, he bought *The Wasteland* sight unseen upon the recommendation of Ezra Pound), his genius as a publisher is beyond dispute.

That is, of course, if such a haughty designation is appropriate to someone who has also been called a "huckster" and has been compared to P. T. Barnum.

Nevertheless, even if Liveright had not published any of these authors, his genius could be solely based on his founding of Modern Library, a series that was the cash cow for both Boni & Liveright and later a new publishing house called "Random House." That the Modern Library still thrives a century later amidst the jungle of the international publishing world is only further evidence of Liveright's publishing genius.

But in spite of being the publisher of writing genius (e.g., Eliot, Faulkner, and Hemingway) and himself a publishing genius (if there ever was one), the movie version of Liveright's life does not reflect this in its title.

However, a recent film that returns to this period of U.S. publishing history does carry this term.

In 1935, the year of release of *The Scoundrel*, the third best-selling book of the year was *Of Time and the River.* It was the second novel of an American writing genius, Thomas Wolfe. The 2016 film *Genius*, directed by Michael Grandage, tells Wolfe's story as well as that of his editor, Maxwell Perkins.

The film, widely panned by critics, is based on A. Scott Berg's book *Max Perkins: Editor of Genius*, winner of the 1978 National Book Award. The subtitle of Berg's book is a double entendre, attributing "genius" to both the editor (Perkins) and the writer (Wolfe). A small-budget film ($17 million), *Genius* was a box-office disaster, bringing in not even one-third ($5.6 million) of its production budget.

Box-office receipts and screenplay and acting issues aside, it is as much a must-see movie for students of the publishing world as its now eighty-year-old predecessor, *The Scoundrel*. It begins with Wolfe (played by Jude Law) presenting the manuscript of *Look Homeward, Angel* (1929) to Perkins (played by Colin Firth). Perkins famously worked with Wolfe to cut 90,000 words from the manuscript—rejected by at least three other publishers—and published it with the press for which he edited, Scribner's. For perspective, consider that the cuts to Wolfe's first novel are almost twice as long as the total length of another novel Perkins edited, F. Scott Fitzgerald's *The Great Gatsby*, which is about 47,000 words long.

The film also dramatizes the story of Wolfe turning in three cartons of unnumbered pages to Perkins, and the editor then shaping Wolfe's 400,000 words into one of the bestsellers of 1935, *Of Time and the River*. Wolfe had a falling-out with Perkins, and left Scribner's to work with the editor Edward Campbell of Harper & Brothers, who wound up editing his three posthumous works: the novels *The Web and the Rock* (1939) and *You Can't Go Home Again* (1940), and the short-story collection, *The Hills Beyond* (1941).

When Wolfe died at the age of thirty-seven, his reputation was as much linked to the efforts of his editor, Perkins, as they were to his own "genius." More recently, Arlyn and Matthew J. Bruccoli reconstructed and published the "author's cut" of *Look Homeward, Angel* in celebration of the centennial of Wolfe's birth, opening up the case that the restored version is superior to the Perkins version.[1]

According to the Bruccoli's, the original version of the novel was 294,000 words, not the 330,000 usually claimed; and Perkins cut 66,000 words, not the 90,000 usually claimed. Moreover, the typescript was not five feet high, but rather "required a little more than two reams of paper—a stack of about 6 inches." But here is the real kicker: "With the same typography and design as the 626-page *Look Homeward, Angel*, it would have made a book of about 825 pages—not impossible to publish in one volume, as this [the Bruccolis'] edition demonstrates. *Gone with the Wind* (1936) had 1,037 pages." It was the best-selling book of both 1936 *and* 1937.

The Bruccolis' quote a 1930 letter from F. Scott Fitzgerald to Maxwell Perkins: "He strikes me as a man who should be let alone as to length, if he has to be published in five volumes." Fitzgerald's letter and the Bruccoli's publication of the "author's cut" of *Look Homeward, Angel* put the work of two literary geniuses at odds with each other: one, the editor of some of the greatest writers in American literary history; the other, the American literary genius who died all too soon. Add to them the contested "genius" of Liveright and a sense of the difficulties of attributing this term to the publishing world emerges.

Mozart did not have an editor who changed his scores after he wrote them, and no one would ever consider the publisher of Einstein's articles on relativity to be a genius. But genius in the world of literary publishing is a much more co-dependent affair.

The ability of publishers to identify new talent from the sea of manuscripts put before them requires a special quality; and the work of some editors with this new talent can rise well above a mere mundane activity. But how does one separate the "genius" of the writer from the work of their editor and their publisher?

The problem here is that publishing genius, that is, the work of publishers and editors, can only be known by the fruits of their work. Namely, the published book.

If the book is a great one, then the authors dance with the term "genius," not the publishing "stage crew." If it is a lousy one, then it is often easier to question the publisher's aptitude and the work of the editor, than to blame the writer. This leaves little room for acknowledgment of publishing genius.

Maybe there were no movies made about publishers after Liveright because of the difficulties of finding genius in their work. And maybe director Grandage's effort to tell the story of an editorial genius flopped because no one (except maybe editors) wants to hear about the efforts of editors in fostering genius.

In the world of imagination, genius needs no editor. And films like *Amadeus* (director Miloš Forman's 1984 masterpiece), which led the viewer to believe that Mozart took dictation from God in composing his scores, keep this myth alive.

But in the real world, writers rely on both publishers and editors to achieve their creative potential. And they know that most publishers are not scoundrels, and that a few of them, such as Horace Liveright, even aspired toward publishing genius. The problem though, as the film *Genius* has recently made abundantly clear, is that publishing genius does *not* make for a very interesting movie.

5

The Writer Who Tried to Save the World

Some authors have great expectations for their books. But who in their right mind expects their book to be able to save the world?

The one-hundredth anniversary of one such book is quickly approaching. Its author is well known as are many of his books, some of which have been adapted into movies. But not this one, that is, unless you want to count a Mel Brooks movie with a similar title.

While some today might have read this author's most ambitious book, they probably number far fewer than a century ago. And though you might have seen it on a dusty shelf in a used bookstore, you probably did not know the high expectations under which it was composed and published.

The author is H. G. Wells—and the book is *Outline of History*.

While often remembered today as a science fiction writer, upon his death in 1946, the New York Times concluded his obituary with the claim that he was the greatest *public teacher* of his time.

The author of over one hundred books, Herbert George Wells, lived through both the First World War and the Second World War, and died at nearly eighty years of age. He was a committed socialist, who wrote in many different genres, including novel, politics, history, textbook, and social commentary. Widely known and admired for his fiction, particularly early science fiction works such as *The Time Machine* (1895), *The Island of Doctor Moreau* (1896), *The Invisible Man* (1897), *The War of the Worlds* (1898), and *The First Men in the Moon* (1901), Wells saw his novels as a way to further his political views.

However, for Wells, this was not enough. He needed to reach, or better yet, *teach* more people. "The novels were useful," writes David Smith, one of his biographers, "at least for Wells as a means of working out his ideas, but they did not reach a wide enough audience."

Also, while one of the early advocates of a League of Nations with whom he helped pen a draft covenant during the First World War, he became, notes Arthur Salter, one of his commentators, "profoundly disappointed in the actual League, which was based upon the inter-state principle and recognized and preserved national sovereignty."

Though Wells followed the birth of the League of Nations closely, he turned and rent on it, continues Salter, "as he had so often turned and rent other institutions which had first roused his hopes and then disappointed him." Still, in spite of his misgivings about the League itself, his political writings have been highly influential, most explicitly on the 1948 Universal Declaration of Human Rights, which was adopted by the United Nations, the postwar successor to the League of Nations. A distinction that puts him in the company of the great German philosopher Immanuel Kant, whose work was also instrumental in the development of the United Nations.

The need to teach the public, particularly in the wake of the First World War, became a priority for Wells. Earlier in his career, he had been a teacher and in fact his first books were textbooks, one on biology and another co-authored one on physiography, both in 1893. Critic David Smith even claims, "Wells never stopped thinking of himself as a teacher." "His earliest work [as a teacher], and his formal training [as a teacher] continued to manifest itself in all of his writing."

The need though to become a public educator and to espouse a philosophy of education became acute after Wells stepped away from the League of Nations. In short, he wanted to produce textbooks as a way to prevent war—or more directly, to save the world. Writes Smith,

> He and his friends on the League of Nations committee had discussed textbooks and methods of education, as a way of preventing further wars, but time did not permit them to produce their own. Wells apparently asked members of the committee, especially Alfred Zimmern, Gilbert Murray, and Ernest Barker, to work on a new world history to replace the older nationalistic and narrow treatments. They refused, on the grounds of lack of time, lack of formal preparation, and unwillingness to give the effort. Wells decided that he must do it himself.

So, around Christmas 1918, Wells and his second wife, Jane, began work on what was to become *The Outline of History: Being a Plain History of Life and*

Mankind, which Smith says is "one of the more significant and widely read books of our century."

It should be noted that in spite of having already written and published over fifty books, including many that we now consider classics of science fiction, Wells' income from these books would only carry him through 1919. His expenses included two children who were in school, another (Anthony West) that he had out of wedlock, and various homes he and his wife owned and maintained.

So, on the surface, writing a history textbook was not a great career move for the established novelist. But thus began the second phase of his writing career, one aimed at him becoming a public educator. "He would devote the years left to him," comments Smith, "to a campaign to educate the world—through textbooks, through speaking, through writing, through travel and through propaganda—in fact, through the very life he lived."

The first edition of *Outline* was researched and composed in late 1918 through late 1919 with the first signatures of the twenty-four part serialized edition of the work appearing in November of 1919. The first edition was reprinted as two volumes in the U.K. in 1920 and then again in 1921 in the U.S. For the next thirty years, Wells did many revisions of the book to incorporate new knowledge and to account for criticisms of it—and there were many.

Though Wells was an established writer, he was not an historian—a fact he openly acknowledged in the book. "The writer is not in any professional sense an historian, but he has been making out his own private Outline from the beginnings of his career," wrote Wells in the "Introduction" to *Outline*. "He has always been preoccupied with history as one whole and with the general forces that make history," he continued. "It is the twist of his mind."

In addition to his wife, Jane, Wells primarily enlisted the help of five others: J. F. Horrabin, an artist; the extraordinary classical scholar, Gilbert Murray; the director of the Museum of Natural History, Sir. E. Ray Lankester; the explorer and cultural anthropologist, Sir Henry H. Johnston; and the political scientist and historian, Ernest Barker. These principals as well as a cast of others read and commented on drafts of the *Outline* through its first publication. Ultimately, though Wells incorporated much of the commentary and criticism he received from others, the book remained and remains the work of an amateur historian.

Outline of History, though, made H. G. Wells a wealthy man. He did not have to worry about income the rest of his life as a result of its publication, and was free to (and did) write whatever he wanted to write without financial consideration. The serialized edition and first two volume editions alone sold over half a million copies, and would come to be translated into many languages. He was even later asked to do two more outlines: one on biology, and another one on sociology, economics, and education, which were published respectively as *The Science of Life: A Summary of Contemporary Knowledge about Life and its Possibilities* (1930) and *The Work, Wealth and Happiness of Mankind* (1932). He also negotiated for some time with Hollywood to produce a film version of *Outline*. The plan was scrapped, though, when Wells refused to add to the *Outline* screenplay, says Salter, a "continuing love interest; a pair of lovers [that] must be miraculously reincarnated in each age and renew their romance."

Though the Mel Brooks movie, *History of the World, Part I* (1981) is not a film adaptation of Wells' *Outline*, it is not a stretch to say that it is influenced by his work. Wells' *Outline of History* launched a new type of historical writing, "world history." Before this book, histories were either regional or periodic. Wells changed all of that with *Outline*, and launched the now commonplace practice of producing and teaching world history.

In Wells and his *Outline of History*, we find a high-profile effort to confront and heal the despair and abandon of a world torn apart by war through the production of a textbook: a textbook aimed at saving the world. According to Norman and Jeanne Mackenzie, co-authors of a biography of Wells, he believed "the war was an educational breakdown . . . and in education lay whatever hope there was for mankind." "He had tried politics; he had tried to reach men's minds through the metaphors of fiction; he had sought to sway public opinion by journalism." "The last hope lay in what had been the first of his occupations," they continue. "He must again become a teacher, but a teacher-at-large to the human race, driven by the immensity and urgency of his new task."

In spite of the historical quality and other infelicities of the *Outline*, there is something very noble about this project. Wells clearly did not write this textbook for the money (even though it did make him rich). He also did not write it as an act of despair (his real despair about the world would only come years later, particularly in his last work, *Mind at the End of its Tether* [1945]) or as a mere report to the academy on a world gone wrong (even though he believed the world as a whole was heading in the wrong direction, the book was written for a popular audience).

He wrote *Outline of History* because he seemed to truly believe in the power of education, and specifically textbooks, to change the attitudes and beliefs of people, if not also change the world. Indeed, he believed that life after the Great War had become a race between education and catastrophe. Writing this textbook was one of the ways he hoped to sway the outcome toward the former rather than the latter.

One hundred years after Wells famously attempted to save the world with a book, we find ourselves similarly poised. Namely, between education and catastrophe. Totalitarianism is again in the air; so too are dictatorships and various forms of oppression; and the war sabers are rattling across the world. Is it time to dust off *Outline* or should we look for new public teachers?

Let's use the one-hundredth anniversary of the publication of H. G. Wells's *Outline* as an opportunity to reflect on what we as writers are doing to confront and heal the despair and abandon in our own time.

6

The End of American Literature

"It was not a street anymore but a world. . . ."

This is the opening line of Don DeLillo's 2007 novel *Falling Man*, but it could also be the opening line of the new millennium.

Bruce Robbins says this sentence can be read as a description of "lower Manhattan in the chaotic minutes after the attack on the World Trade Center on September 11, 2001." But so too, he continues, can it "also be read as a description of *Falling Man* itself, and perhaps of the contemporary American novel in general." "So read," resumes Robbins, "the sentence would suggest that the American novel has recently become more worldly, whether because of 9/11 or in response to larger causes that 9/11 stands in for."

While Robbins calls this proposition "gently self-congratulatory, hence open to doubt," still he says "there are also reasons for taking it seriously." And Robbins, and many other critics of late have taken this proposition very seriously. So seriously in fact that some contend that "American literature" would be more accurately phrased "American *world* literature."

Christian Moraru, for example, argues that the phrase "American world literature" "calls on us to listen carefully, in the phrase itself, for the rustle and rumors of worldliness in the U.S. and vice versa." "Should we do so," says Moraru, "we might further wonder: Is this literature a worldly thematics, literature 'about the world' rather than about 'us' ('US'), about the 'American world'? Or, is American literature becoming a subset of world literature?"

While seeing the world on the street of lower Manhattan amidst the chaos of the World Trade Center attacks, and finding the world or "worldliness" in greater degrees in post-9/11 American fiction is one way to read the phrase "American world literature," it would not be the kind of change that occurred "on or about September 2001."

This change is not merely a shift to a more "worldly" (or global, international, cosmopolitan, transnational, and so on) thematic in American fiction, as each of these can be convincingly traced back to various works and authors in the history of the American novel, if not back to its very "invention" (to borrow the term used by Paul Giles). The change that occurred "on or about September 2001" is more substantial and the break with the past potentially more radical.

To view this change and see better its break with the past, one needs to go back not to New York City on September 11, 2001, but rather to Cambridge, Massachusetts, on August 31, 1837. For it was on this date that Ralph Waldo Emerson walked onto the stage of American life, declaring, "[t]he world is nothing, the man is all." It was an entry that arguably set American literature on its *nonworldly* course.

Much like 2001, 1837 was not just any year in American history. Rather, it was, by some accounts, "the worst year the United States of America had ever experienced." "Society," writes Emerson in his journals in May of 1837, "has played out its last stake; it is checkmated. Young men have no hope. Adults stand like daylaborers idle in the streets. None calleth us to labor. The old wear no crown of warm light on their grey hairs. The present generation is bankrupt of principles & hope, as of property." This leaves Emerson to wonder aloud, "Is the world sick?"

By August of 1837, the month Emerson steps onto the stage of American life, says literary historian Larzer Ziff, "the price of cotton had fallen by almost one half; mobs had demonstrated repeatedly in the streets of New York and, in response to the inflated prices of food and fuel, had looted the city's flour warehouses; the major banks had suspended specie payments; and the sale of public lands in the West had fallen by some 82 percent." Add to this the fact that since 1790, the first year of the U.S. Census, the number of people in the United States subject to slavery was increasing by approximately 30 percent per year, with approximately 2 million slaves in 1830 and 2.5 million by 1840, the United States was in pretty rough shape in August of 1837, compelling Emerson to conclude in his journal, "The world has failed."

With slavery in full swing and American morale in ruins as a result of the panic of 1837, Emerson was asked to give the annual Phi Beta Kappa address at Harvard University the day following commencement. But he was not the first choice, and was asked only after the Reverend Dr. Wainwright had been invited by Cornelius Felton, a professor of Greek at Harvard, but declined.

Emerson, Felton's second choice, was an underwhelming one, to say the least. Not only was Emerson merely an honorary member of Phi Beta Kappa, he was not even the second choice for class poet. And though he had anonymously published his first book, *Nature*, the previous year, it was on the whole unenthusiastically received.

Nevertheless, the thirty-four-year-old Emerson had lofty expectations for his oration, writing in his journals before the event, "Let me begin anew. Let me teach the finite to know its Master. Let me ascend above my fate and work down upon my world." Though he believes the world in which he lives is "sick" and has "failed," he nonetheless looks forward to addressing this sickness and failure. "The black times have a great scientific value," writes Emerson in his journal. "It is an epoch so critical a philosopher would not miss."

The theme of his oration, "The American Scholar," was a conventional one for the annual Phi Beta Kappa address since Emerson was a boy, and it does not appear that he struggled much in writing it. Nevertheless, in spite of its conventional theme, what Emerson said was far from conventional. Delivered a little more than sixty years after the United States declared its political independence, it was a call for the United States to forge its own literary traditions and history. Emerson's oration was regarded by observers at the time as our declaration of *intellectual* independence—one that still resonates with us to this day.

"Events, actions arise, that must be sung, that will sing themselves," said Emerson. "Who can doubt that poetry will revive and lead in a new age, as the star in the constellation Harp, which now flames in our zenith, astronomers announce, shall one day be the polestar for a thousand years." He reminds his audience that the commencement of their "literary year" is long on "hope" but short on "labor." "We do not meet for games of strength or skill, for the recitation of histories, tragedies, and odes, like the ancient Greeks; for parliaments of love and poesy, like the Troubadours; nor for the advancement of science, like our contemporaries in the British and European capitals," comments Emerson.

> Thus far, our holiday has been simply a friendly sign of the survival of the love of letters amongst a people too busy to give to letters any more. . . . Perhaps the time is already come when it ought to be, and will be, something else; when the sluggard intellect of this continent will look from under its iron lids and fill the postponed expectation of the world with something better than the exertions of mechanical skill. Our day of

> dependence, our long apprenticeship to the learning of other lands, draws to a close. The millions that around us are rushing into life, cannot always be fed on the sere remains of foreign harvests.

Though Emerson was not waiving the flag on August 31, 1837, he was imploring the audience for the formation of a unique and distinct national literature. "We have," said Emerson, "listened too long to the courtly muses of Europe."

But he was not the first. Literary journals going back twenty-five years were sprinkled with similar pleas. Still, the distinguished audience of the Phi Beta Kappa Society was not expecting it. Emerson was merely speaking on the traditional topic of the conference, and was by far not the most prominent person to date to speak on it. Nevertheless, at the conclusion of his oration, James Russell Lowell said it was "an event without any former parallel in our literary annals," and Oliver Wendell Holmes called it "our Intellectual Declaration of Independence."

Emerson continued to voice his revolt against his times from 1837 to 1844 in a series of occasional addresses to writers, scholars, and the clergy at meetings of library associations, convocations of literary societies, commencement ceremonies, and sponsored evening lectures at public halls. In these addresses, he was clear and defiant, and his intent was to shock his audience. "Amidst a planet peopled with conservatives," said Emerson, "one Reformer may yet be born."

It is important to recall Emerson's call for a unique and distinct national literature amidst a sick and failing world because today we sit on the cusp of calling for its opposite, namely, a non-national literature. Is this not what we mean when we employ the phrase "American world literature"? But as Stanley Cavell so brilliantly notes in *This New Yet Unapproachable America: Lectures after Emerson after Wittgenstein* (1989), Emerson was not simply advocating that we turn our backs on Europe and the world, but rather addressing the *poverty* of American philosophy.

"Others take Emerson to advise America to ignore Europe," writes Cavell, but "to me his practice means that part of the task of discovering philosophy in America is discovering terms in which it is given to us to inherit the philosophy of Europe." "Its legacy may hardly look like philosophy at all," continues Cavell, "but perhaps rather like an odd development of literature."

But didn't we on or around September 2001 discover just the opposite, namely, that the tables are now reversed? That instead of the issue of how much America should inherit from Europe (and the rest of the world) and on what terms, the issue is now one of how much Europe (and the rest of the world) should inherit from America—and on what terms. Isn't this the logical conclusion of America's rise to global power and prestige?

Cavell sets the condition of American philosophy not as one of seeking *independence* from Europe, so much as one of being in a condition of *poverty*. "Poverty as a condition of philosophy is hardly a new idea," comments Cavell. "Emerson deploys it as an idea specifically of America's deprivations, its bleakness and distance from Europe's achievements, as constituting America's necessity, and its opportunity, for finding itself." However, when the towers fell and we realized our streets are "a world," Americans could no longer claim poverty as the condition of their philosophy.

One-percent wealth and the neoliberal pursuit of it now is the condition of American philosophy in the new millennium. Emerson, as Cavell reminds us, implored us to hold hard to our poverty. "The poverty that," writes Cavell, "morally speaking, is pleasing to the God and affords us access to the humanity of others—it is its poverty, not its riches, that constitutes America's claim upon others—is, philosophically speaking, our access to necessity, our route out of privacy."

No longer, though, can the United States, the wealthiest country on earth, claim poverty as its access to the humanity of others. The tables are now turned: on or about September 2001, the riches of America, not its poverty, constitute its claim on others—or, perhaps, their claim on us. Osama Bin Laden positions himself on the side of an impoverished world and taunts us with our new God, "Gold Almighty," while claiming for his group, terrorists, what is pleasing to the God.

On or about September 11, 2001, American literature ended as dramatically as it began. We lost our independence from the world when the towers came crashing down; we also lost national literature to a world now occupying our streets.

In retrospect, our philosophical and literary independence has been squandered in the pursuit of increasingly destructive forms of capitalism. An act of terrorism brought to the fore that our wealth and prosperity may be denying us access to the humanity of others. The world stood at the footsteps of neoliberal America—and demanded change.

7

Digital Fatigue

The days of mourning the death of the printed book may finally be drawing to a close. After ten years of electronic euphoria in the book world, we may be seeing some signs of digital fatigue.

This does not mean though that the musty used bookstores and soulless chain retailers that have slowly but steadily disappeared from our towns and cities will soon reopen. It would take nothing less than a complete collapse of the internet to derail the dominance of book shopping online. The prices are too good and the selection too vast for the brick-and-mortar bookstore to be effectively anything more than a showroom for books purchased online.

Still, the number of independent bookstores in the United States has *risen* over the past eight years, not decreased.

In 2009, there were 1,401 independent bookstore companies in the United States with 1,651 different locations. Over the next seven years, both the number of companies and the number of locations have increased every year—increased to the point where, in 2016, there are 1,775 independent bookstore companies in the United States with 2,311 different locations, more than any in the preceding eight-year period.[2] So, while the chains like Barnes & Noble and Hastings may be struggling or worse, the independents are on the rise.

Nor does this nascent digital fatigue mean a gross reduction in the total number of ebooks. Each year thousands of new titles are released by both traditional and nontraditional publishers. Also, older titles are becoming increasingly available through initiatives such as the Google Print Library Project. Launched in December of 2004, three months after Google Print itself was announced as a joint program with some of the major presses in the world, the Library Project was announced as one with some of the major libraries of the world. The following year, Google Print was renamed Google Books, which more than ten years later has become a major repository for ebooks.

Still, the Google Books project is a poster child for the fatigue of the digital book revolution. Ten years ago, Google aimed within ten years to have publicly available through Google Books all of the world's books. Its completion would mean that Google Books would have scanned all of the world's books and that they would all be completely available online to the public—at no cost.

To date, though Google Books contains an impressive 30 million volumes, most of the titles are inaccessible or only come through in snippets of text. To get a sense of the size of Google Books, consider that the Library of Congress contains around 37 million volumes. But the failure of the Google Books initiative has little to do with the size of its collection, which is already impressive, or people tiring of using digital books. Rather, the issue was one of how to deal with copyrights, use permission, and, ultimately, compensation to authors and publishers.

In 2002, Google was scanning everything under the sun thinking that everyone would be happy with the idea that all books would in time be freely accessible to anyone with digital access. After years of haggling, a settlement was reached in 2008 with authors, publishers, and Google to make the collection available to the public for pay. However, in 2011, the 2008 settlement was thrown out by a federal judge. The task of sorting out the copyright issues was then handed to Congress, who to this day has not yet sorted them out.

If you are curious as to how far Google was from its aim of digitizing all of the books in the world, Leonid Taycher, a software engineer who worked on the Google Books project gave a precise figure in 2010: 129,864,880. So, assuming that the programs written by the Google engineers were somewhat accurate in their estimations of the total number of extant books worldwide, Google Books is about 100 million titles away from their goal of 130 million.

The failure of Google Books to achieve their goal of scanning and making all of the world's books available online aside, there are more ebooks available today than at any other time in history. This in itself is no small achievement. And Google Books remains a major resource for scholars and the public alike.

Still, the majority of *new* books published as ebooks are self-published. In 2010, there were 38,763 self-published ebooks. By comparison, by June of 2010, Google Books reported having already scanned 12 million books.

In 2011 and 2012, the numbers of self-published books published as ebooks rose again to 88,238 and 158,493. However, in 2013, the number dropped off to

156,058 though rose again in 2014 to 172,511. But again, the number dropped off the next year, with 153,160 self-published ebooks produced in 2015.

This fluctuation or drop off might not be so interesting if it were not coupled with a steady *increase* in self-published *print* books. Over the same six-year period, self-published print book production has *significantly* increased every year. Thus, compared to the increases in self-published print books, the flattening and decrease in self-published ebooks appear as a sign of digital fatigue.

In 2010, there were 114,215 self-published print books and each succeeding year this number rose: 158,972 in 2011; 235,639 in 2012; 304,006 in 2013; 427,210 in 2014; and in 2015 a mind-boggling 573,965 self-published print books were released.

These figures are important because compared to traditional publishing, self-publishing dominates the publishing world today. The vast majority of new titles being published today are self-published.

To get a sense of the numbers here, consider that, in 2012, there were 309,957 traditional publications and 2,042,840 *nontraditional* publications. While some of these nontraditional publications were reprints, print-on-demand, and wiki-based materials, we know that at least *394,132* of these over two million titles were self-published. A number that clearly exceeds the 309,957 traditional publications that year.

It is not a large leap to assume that many more were self-published albeit not through traceable venues such as the self-publishing companies' figures that generated the 394,132 number cited above. However, just based on the output of self-publishing companies, since 2010, self-published books have increased over 375 percent, and from 2014 to 2015 self-publishing has grown over 21 percent. But one figure says it all: in 2010, there were 152,978 ISBNs assigned to self-published titles, whereas in 2015 the number had increased almost fivefold to 727,125 ISBNs.

Whether one is impressed with the growth figures in self-publishing, what is to be noticed here is that the preferred medium for self-published titles is the print book. Again, just look at the recent numbers: 573,965 self-published print books to 153,160 self-published ebooks in 2015.

Self-published print titles outpaced ebooks almost four to one.

In fact, Bowker, who is a major source of data on publishing and self-publishing in the United States has also said that part of the appeal of print books over ebooks to self-published authors is that print books enable them "to reach a broad audience, often via independent bookstores."

Combine then the rise in independent bookstores over the past eight years with the rapid increase of self-published print books, and you have the makings of a Good News story for print-book culture—amidst claims that it was dead and buried long ago.

But the evidence of a resurgence of print books over ebooks does not end with the fact that self-published authors today prefer print books to ebooks. Readers too seem increasingly to prefer print book (pbook) technology to its digital competition.

A recent study by the Pew Research Center reports that ebook reading has flattened over the past three years, whereas pbook reading is rising—and is still much more popular than ebook reading.

The Pew Research Center Report on book reading says that, in 2011, in spite of over 12 million books being available online, only 17 percent of its respondents claimed to have read an ebook, whereas 71 percent claimed to have read a print book. The very next year, ebook reading rose, while pbook reading declined with 23 percent claiming to have read an ebook and 65 percent claiming to have read a print book.

But it's the figures over the next three years that are the most remarkable ones. In spite of the considerable increases in the overall number of ebooks available for reading, ebook reading has peaked and flattened over the past three years. In 2014, 28 percent of respondents said that they had read an ebook. The next year the percentage dropped a percentage point and in 2016 it rose again to its 2014 percentage. However, by comparison, pbook reading rose to 69 percent in 2014, dipped to 63 percent in 2015, and then rose again to its 2012 rate of 65 percent in 2016.

This means that over the past six years, ebook reading has increased 11 percent but pbook reading has only dipped 6 percent. These figures could explain why the overwhelming majority of self-published books in 2015 were pbooks. Reason: over *twice as many people today have read a print book in the past year than have read an ebook.*

If you are a prospective author, and you know this to be the case and want your book to be read, then you would be foolish to self-publish it as an ebook as opposed to a pbook. Twice as many readers today prefer pbooks to ebooks. But further findings of the study only strengthen the case for pbooks over ebooks—or, more modestly, attest to the presence of some form of digital fatigue.

The Pew study also reported that while nearly four in ten Americans read print books exclusively, only 6 percent are digital-only book readers. Additionally, more Americans read print books than either read ebooks or listen to audio books.

Another surprising finding of the study is that 80 percent of 18- to 29-year olds read a book in 2015 as compared to 67 percent of those 65 and older. And while the young folks are more likely to read books in a digital format, they are also more likely to read print books as well. The Pew study finds 61 percent of seniors to have read a print book in 2015 as compared to 72 percent of young adults.

Reports like this one from the Pew Research Center fly in the face of others that indicate that ebook sales are rising annually. So in spite of the fact that it is estimated today that more than 30 percent of all new book sales are ebooks, and that ebook sales have risen from 63 million in 2008, the year after the introduction of the Kindle Reader, to 512 million in 2013, print books remain the reading object of choice.

Ten years ago the fear was that e-readers were going to render obsolete print books. During the same period, Google was going to render libraries obsolete by digitizing every book in the world—and making them freely accessible to the public.

Pushing the clock forward, we see that not only was the release of the first Kindle readers by Amazon in the fall of 2007 not the beginning of the end of print reading and print books, but that the allure of the printed word remains relatively stable during the first decade of the digital book revolution.

The real changes in the first decade of the ebook revolution are not so much in reading habits but rather in the way we acquire books and publish them. Sure it is great to freely access titles through Google Books. But soon you find that most of the titles are missing key pages and not fully accessible.

In its current state, the Google Books library is effectively a library of "damaged" books. A library of books with pages "torn out" or "missing"; a library of books not even fit for the remainder tables of yore.

Digital fatigue comes not only from waiting for the U.S. Congress to sort out the legal and financial issues underlying Google Books but also from having to deal with online access to bits and pieces of 30 million books. Few acts of reading today are more frustrating than locating a Google Book only to learn that some of the pages that you want to read are not available for your use.

If brick-and-mortar bookstores have become a sort of showroom for online bookstores, then Google's online library has become a showroom for brick-and-mortar libraries.

Couple the shortcomings of Google Books with the steady reemergence of the independent bookstore over the past eight years and the current reading habit figures, and you have a digital book world that seems to have much less energy and momentum than it had a decade ago.

What we do have though that is energizing and motivated is a growing legion of authors who are leveraging the digital revolution to self-publish their work—and to opt out of traditional publishing.

The post-Kindle world has become one where electronic euphoria has finally given way to a form of digital fatigue.

It is enough to render some of the digital visionaries blind and awaken print books from the land of the dead.

8

The Three Percent

"It's all Greek to me!" It's a well-known, kneejerk idiom indicating a lack of comprehension.

But what if it were literally true? What if someone walked up and started speaking to you in a foreign language? Or handed you a book in a language unknown to you and suggested that you read it?

Would you say "It's all Greek to me!" and hand the book back? Or would you look for a means to puzzle out the text?

It's a simple test of our level of commitment to multilingualism and multiculturalism, asking how much we value world literature and how far would we go to welcome it.

To be sure, no one in the world can speak or understand every language. But the gauge of our commitment to multilingualism and multiculturalism is not our ability speak or read every language. Rather, it is our reaction to languages, literatures, and cultures that are unknown to us.

If we are committed to multiculturalism and world literature, then the first order of business is to eradicate the "It's all Greek to me!" attitude.

In Europe alone, there are 235 living languages. But living European languages represent only 3 percent of living languages worldwide. If you assumed it was significantly higher than 3 percent, then perhaps you suffer from "Eurocentrism." To cure it, one need only turn one's gaze toward Africa, Asia, and the Americas.

Countries in the Americas, including the Caribbean, have nearly 1,000 living languages, which make up just over 14 percent of languages worldwide. However, the majority of living languages are divided between the countries in Africa, which have 2,110 or just over 30 percent of living languages worldwide, and the countries of Asia, which have 2,332 or nearly 34 percent of the living languages worldwide.

Of the living languages worldwide, English is one of 6,909. And this does not even consider dead languages such as Latin and Aramaic.

While some of these languages are used by a relatively small number of people, others are not. Consider some of the many living languages of India: over 65 million people speak Tamil, nearly 68 million speak Marathi, and nearly 70 million converse in Telugu.

Or look to Pakistan, where over 78 million people speak Lahnda.

And though English is by far spoken in more countries worldwide than any other language (112), more people worldwide speak Spanish (329 million) than English (328 million). Still, both of these languages are dwarfed by the number of people who speak Chinese worldwide (1.2 billion).

"It's all Greek to me" was our way of expressing that there are things that are beyond our understanding. It was not meant to demean Greek or other languages nor was it meant to indicate that what is being said is nonsense. Still, it signified a kind of giving up on language and understanding. It said, others might know what is going on here, but I'm not one of them.

The phrase is not fit for a world where international affairs are increasingly everyone's affair. Where acts of violence and hatred are often found at the crossroads of differing cultures and languages. Where a bombing in one part of the world has connections to many other parts of the world. Where a shooting in America ripples around the globe.

Ours cannot be a world where people simply give up seeking understanding or caring when it is apparent that a language or culture is beyond their ken. But neither can we all be expected to become experts in every language or understand every culture. Learning even just one language is a task that usually involves years of dedication and study—and cultural understanding is no less difficult to achieve. Between the two extremes—ignorance and intellection—lies the middle-way: translation.

Instead of giving up on understanding what is being communicated in a language that is unknown to us or devoting years of study to mastering it to the point where we do understand what is being communicated, we seek the helping hand of translation, namely, the act of bringing a statement or text from one language into another.

But translation is a slow business. One needs more than just a mastery of the original language of the text and the language of the translation. Language is rooted in culture and it is the ability to negotiate this relationship that often makes one translation work better than another. Translation, especially of literary works, is more complicated than merely finding a semantic correlation between words, sentences, and paragraphs. One seeks something more, and it is in this something more that translation becomes as much an art and work of artistry as the original.

In many ways, our commitment to translation is a good barometer of our commitment to the global community and international affairs. Again, it is unreasonable, even in an increasingly global community, to expect people to master multiple languages and cultures as a means of gaining an understanding of the world outside of one's language or languages.

While no one should be discouraged from learning one or ten additional languages, the expectation as a necessary condition of cultural understanding is too high in a world that needs more understanding now. Moreover, to posit incommensurability between languages may be theoretically possible, but is practically imprudent. Incommensurability creates walls; what the world needs now are more bridges.

What does it say then about our commitment to global understanding and multicultural awareness when we learn that only 3 percent of books published in the U.S. are translations? This often-stated figure is the real indicator of our commitment to global relations and world literature.

Consider the following: in 2013, there were 542 translations published in the United States with 449 of them being works of fiction.[3] This may seem a large number until one considers that over 50,000 works of fiction were published in the U.S. in 2013. This puts the number of translations published in the U.S. at about 1 percent just among works of fiction, which is of course a much smaller number than the total number of books published in the U.S. in 2013—a number that was estimated to be over 1.4 million.

Moreover, support of translation by corporate publishing as opposed to independent and small presses is embarrassingly low. In 2013, Penguin published 13 translations, Knopf published 5, and Random House only 2. By comparison, Dalkey Archive, a small press, published 41.

Does this mean that a small press is more committed to global understanding and bringing the literature of the world to an English-speaking audience than a publishing corporation with billions of dollars in revenue? Or that Dalkey Archive has a larger role in the dissemination of translations than Penguin Random House, a company that publishes one in four books worldwide?

Another 28 translations were published in 2013 by AmazonCrossing, a subsidiary of the book-distributing giant Amazon, which is slowly entering the publishing market.

To be sure, this is the same Amazon whose Kindle Reader paved the way for the growth of the ebook and whose online store played a key role in the demise of the independent bookstore. It is also the same company that recently locked horns with Hachette and its authors over pre-sales revenue. Thus, if the past is prologue to the future, then Amazon's entry in the world of translation needs to be closely watched.

Nonetheless, independent and small presses continue to be vital to the translation world and world literature in the same way that they are vital to innovative writing and heterodox thinking. Namely, without them, contemporary translation and narrative innovation would virtually disappear from the publishing scene.

The number of translations published in the United States reveals both the relative lack of interest by corporate publishing in translation and the relatively large interest in translation by independent presses. Roughly speaking, 1 out of 5 translations in 2013 was done by a corporate publisher, whereas 4 out of 5 were done by an independent or small press.[4]

In October of 2015, Amazon invested $10 million into AmazonCrossing, which since 2010 has published 200 translations of authors from 29 countries writing in 19 languages. The translations are offered in print and digital, and in some cases even audio format. According to Amazon, the investment is a "commitment over the next five years to increase the number and diversity of books in translation."

If we have learned anything about the entry of Amazon into areas of the book business it is that things usually get worse in that area before they get better. For example, though Amazon was the final blow for hundreds of independent bookstores in the United States, there are signs that the independent bookstore is having a comeback.

In the case of Amazon's entry into the translation publishing business, while there have been complaints about translator compensation rates and the quality of AmazonCrossing translations, these issues are not uncommon ones in this area of publishing. The real issue is whether Amazon's entry marks a significant improvement in this area or not.

In 2014, the number of translations published in the United States increased to 600 from 542 the previous year with AmazonCrossing contributing 46 of them. Then, in 2015, the overall number of translations published in the United States fell to 549 with AmazonCrossing contributing a whopping 75 to the year's total.

Though the sample here is small, we are already seeing signs of the Amazon Effect. Its "get big fast" business philosophy in an area as small as translation publishing, coupled with annual financial revenues that were set at 107 billion in 2015, means that the translation world and everyone who cares about the dissemination of world literature needs to pay close attention to AmazonCrossing.

To get some perspective on Amazon's 107 billion, consider that Random House, the world's largest trade publisher, set 2015 sales revenue at 3.7 billion Euros, which today is about 4.1 billion U.S. dollars. Consider as well that the *entire* U.S. publishing industry revenue for 2014 was *only* 28 billion. In other words, Amazon is a giant among publishing giants.

Given that translation is for most their only door into world literature and its role in supporting multiculturalism and global understanding, and given that Amazon has put $10 million on the table to increase their translation endeavors, there is every reason to believe that in the years to come, translation's 3 percent will be increasingly dominated by AmazonCrossing.

However, what should not be expected is for translation as an overall percentage of U.S. publishing to rise as a result Amazon's entry into the area of translation publishing. This will have to be left to others.

Finally, just as Amazon hastened the rise of digital publishing and drove independent bookstores to near extinction, don't be surprised if small and independent presses who publish translation begin to hear more regularly AmazonCrossing's footsteps behind everything they do. Let's only hope that they are just footsteps—and not a boot to their neck.

9

The Corporate Showroom

Some of the predator-prey tales from bibliographic oceans are well known. Like the one about how the big bookstores ate the little bookstores. Corporate chains such as Borders and Barnes & Noble with their fancy furniture and coffee bars drove many of the independent bookstores to ruin.

But then came along an even bigger fish called Amazon.

This bigger fish accounts for about 40 percent of the book market and has an insatiable appetite for its competition. First it ate through the large corporate chains and is now working its way through the smaller ones.

Borders is long gone—and Barnes & Noble is as good as gone.

In the first quarter of 2016, Barnes & Noble, the largest bookstore chain in the country, reported net losses of almost $35 million from its website and retail stores. The same quarter a year earlier it reported losses of almost $29 million. While a number of things are eating away at its revenue including store closings and losses from its Nook digital unit, the competition from online retailer Amazon is relentless and will not stop until Barnes & Noble folds.

So what does Barnes & Noble plan to do to slow down Amazon's appetite for brick-and-mortar bookstore destruction? Work on its book inventory? Increase customer service? Not even close.

According to its new chief executive, Ronald Boire, in order to stop the bleeding of revenue loses, Barnes & Noble needs to make its stores more attractive and focus more attention on toys, games, and other nonbook merchandise as a key part of its business plan.

Toys? Really? That's the plan?

The chances that Amazon will choke on one of Barnes & Noble's toys and leave it alone are about as likely as Border's reopening its doors. Not only does

Amazon also sell toys and games but, for that matter, it sells just about anything else that can be put in a box and delivered to your doorstep.

Not to mention that another bookstore chain recently failed using the same strategy.

Two years ago, Hastings Entertainment supposedly received a second lease on life when it was sold to Draw Another Circle. The company, which currently has nearly 4,000 employees and a debt of about $139 million, will permanently close all of its stores by Halloween.

Though Hastings Entertainment stores did not do a lot of beautification after their acquisition by Draw Another Circle, they did increase their stock of toys, games, collectibles, and other merchandise. As a result, the amount of retail space in the stores dedicated to books reached an all-time low over the past two years. It was replaced by a wide assortment of merchandise, including hobby items such as model airplanes and cars and sports paraphernalia such as Peyton Manning bobble-heads and Chicago Cubs shot glasses.

With stock like Metallica t-shirts and lava lamps, Hastings came to look more like Spencer Gifts than a bookstore. The books that they did stock were a limited assortment of new titles overpowered by a motley and random assortment of used and sale books. Their policy was to buy back any book with an ISBN—and their stock reflected it. Given the sad state of their inventory, it would not be surprising to learn that books were the least sold items in the store's final years.

And even the folks who did go to Hastings for its books, sometimes even ended up purchasing them elsewhere.

"We don't buy a lot here," said one Hasting's customer, "but it's nice to browse." "A lot of people know that there are better deals on the internet so they buy on Amazon instead of in the store," added the customer. "And I do that too," she said. "I see a book that's $14 and I know I can get it used on Amazon for like a penny."

So if people don't go to chain bookstores to buy books anymore, what then is the future of big bookstore chains such as Barnes & Noble? While toys and games might sell better than books these days, it is not going save a business dedicated to selling books. This is especially true when its customers only go to these stores to buy toys and "window shop" for books that they then go home (or immediately to their cell phone) and order online.

Perhaps Barnes & Noble just needs to bite the bullet and do away with selling books and focus instead on being an upscale toy store with a coffee bar?

Recent statements from its new chief executive and the recent efforts of Hastings make this more than just a fantasy.

It seems the only thing keeping Barnes & Noble afloat these days are the bookstores they run for universities. But won't students too get wise and order their books from the internet if they can find them for a better price? Some universities are even required to tell their students that while they can purchase their books in the university bookstore, they may want to also consider purchasing them online as there is a chance they can find them at a lower price.

In view then of the decline and fall of the independent bookstore and the continued demise of bookstore chains, one would think that Amazon had accomplished its aim. Namely, making brick-and-mortar bookstores obsolete by offering better selection and prices online. Why then after conquering the world of bookselling with ecommerce is Amazon starting to open brick-and-mortar bookstores? Have they lost their mind? Or are they just adding insult to injury by opening stores in the self-same cities where they drove other bookstores out of business?

There has been a lot of speculation on their intentions every since the first Amazon Books opened in early November of 2015 in Seattle. Is the store just an advertising or publicity stunt by Amazon or do they really expect it to be a profitable business? With new locations on tap in Portland, San Diego, and Chicago the questions only continue.

For one thing, the wrong question to ask is whether the stores are going to be more profitable than the brick-and-mortar stores of companies like Borders, Barnes & Noble, and Hastings. Why? Because even if they are not, it does not matter. Amazon is already the largest bookseller in America and short of an ecommerce miracle by another company, they are going to be in this position for a very long time.

Just like their foray into translation, one need go no deeper into the rationale for their bookstore venture than to see it as a marketing strategy. And just as they can afford to put millions of dollars into publishing literature translations without ever expecting to recoup their investment let alone make a profit on them, so too can they open a few high-cost brick-and-mortar bookstores without ever expecting these stores to turn a profit.

Their aim in both endeavors is nothing more or less than to increase the visibility of their brand and the prestige of their company. All with an eye—or smile—toward further dominating the ecommerce market.

It is fitting that the creepy smile of the Amazon logo lacks ears and eyes as it serves as a continuous reminder of their self-satisfaction in devouring their competition without any consideration to how others regard it. Amazon sees no evil in its market domination; and hears no evil in its corporate strategies. It just continuously smiles in dehumanizing neoliberal satisfaction.

It is not that Amazon knows more about the business of brick-and-mortar bookselling than Borders, Barnes & Noble, and Hastings. In fact, their bookstores even betray some common wisdom about book merchandising. For example, the aisles in their Seattle stores are too narrow, making it hard to see the books on the bottom rows without bumping your bottom against another customer.

Also, Amazon Books displays its eye level and lower books face out instead of spine out (books on upper shelves are spine out and for overstock only). This arrangement is a highly inefficient use of merchandise space as it limits book display to only five or so titles per three-foot shelf instead of three to four times that number. Presumably, the face-out display practices of Amazon Books mimics the digital display of books on their website, and aims to afford their physical bookstore one of its most obvious iconic relations to its digital bookstore—and locus of business activity.

My favorite oddity, though, from Amazon's new bookstore is that the personal comments in front of featured books are generated by computers rather than handwritten. Common independent bookstore wisdom is that staff members select some their favorite titles in the store. A handwritten placard is then displayed in front of the book with the staff member's comments as to why it is a good read. However, in Amazon Books, this is not done. Rather, reviews of the book come from online comments about the book on Amazon.com. One also finds Amazon "star ratings" of the books and a proclivity to select groups of books for display according to their high-star ratings in the Seattle store. For example, one display is entitled "High Rated Debut Novels / 4.5 Stars & Above." Another, "Start a New Series / 4.5 Stars & Above."

I don't know if you are like me, but I tend to ignore the comments written by the staff of independent bookstores. While it is nice to see, for example, that one of the staff likes say Robert Pirsig's *Zen and the Art of Motorcycle Maintenance* (a perennial bookstore staff favorite), the comments are not as important to me as is the acknowledgment implied from the handwritten placard that the bookstore staff care about books and have read some of the books that are sold in the store. This was always a distinguishing feature of independent bookstores from the chains whose staff seemed wholly clueless about books in general.

But printing out comments from the internet and displaying them in front of books along with consumer popularity numbers (or "star ratings" in the Amazon vernacular) is just as disrespectful and dehumanizing to the staff of the store as not putting any comments on the books. Both imply that the staff does not have any comments to share or that the store prefers to ignore them. The irony here is that at least in the Seattle store, the staff of Amazon Books *is* highly qualified to make such comments.

Amazon recruited through LinkedIn booksellers and librarians from across the city. The starting wage is $18 per hour and the job comes with benefits. So, while the staff of Amazon Books in Seattle is fairly paid and knowledgeable about books, denying them their book blurbs betrays Amazon's real intention in opening this bookstore. Namely, not to rehumanize bookselling or reestablish brick-and-mortar bookselling as a viable endeavor but rather something far darker: to drive you back to their online bookstore.

Everything about Amazon Books leads you back to the digital world of bookselling. From the internet comments and star ratings displayed in front of the books to the way books are priced and how sales transactions are recorded. Though there are no price reductions displayed on any of the books in the store, customers know that the price of the books in the store is the same price that they are being sold on Amazon.com. So, to get the price, they must go to Amazon.com. Moreover, all books purchased in Amazon Books automatically become part of the customers purchasing history on Amazon.com. Creepy, huh?

Overall, the bookstores that Amazon are opening are based on a very different business model than the bookstores that they put out of business. Whereas the chain bookstores and the independents were set up so that you could find a book in their store, purchase, and take it home all in one visit, Amazon Books seems to be set up more for window shopping than brick-and-mortar purchasing. Not only is the stock very limited because of the way books are displayed but there seems to be not much effort to even simulate the experience of one-stop book shopping. The idea of the store seems to be to whet your appetite for real book shopping, which of course can be had online at Amazon.com, the largest and most comprehensive bookstore in history.

While there is a temptation to say that Amazon Books has more in common with the M&M and Hershey stores in Times Square than a Borders or Barnes & Noble franchise from strip-mall America, this is probably wrongheaded.

The Hershey and M&M stores magnify the shopping experience for lovers of their chocolate confections. They take a simple and singular product, the Hershey bar and the M&M candy, and package and repackage it in a variety of unique ways. These stores celebrate a product that is probably sold in more stores in America than just about any other product aside from Coca-Cola and Marlboro cigarettes. They are one part nostalgia and one part fun. They attract large crowds not because of the uniqueness of the product they sell (Hershey's chocolate bars and M&M's candy) but because of its ubiquity.

In contradistinction to the Hershey and M&M stores, the Amazon stores contain but a small fraction of their product. The one in Seattle was even said to not stock literature's equivalent of the Hershey bar, George Orwell's *Nineteen-Eighty-Four.* Like the Hershey and M&M stores, the Amazon Stores evoke nostalgia albeit more for books and bookstores, rather than youth and days gone by.

But in no way are they fun or silly. The only joy emanating from the Amazon Stores comes from the smile on the Amazon logo. If anything, these stores are scary and horrifying, particularly to anyone who loves good books and great bookstores. And if they are meant to be product showrooms, they are not very good ones.

Amazon Books is more about giving Amazon.com customers a chance to celebrate the success of the company than about selling books or celebrating them. Customers finally get a chance to walk the halls of Amazon with their feet rather than just their browser. While it is tempting to call them "bookstore showrooms," following the comments of the Hastings customer above, this would be wrong. Not only are the prices the same in the physical bookstore as the virtual bookstore, the physical bookstore "shows" but a fraction of the company's products—and only the highest rated ones at that. To be sure, a proper "showroom" would require a much larger stock than they currently offer.

In the end, Amazon Books is a place where visitors can learn more about and celebrate the largest and most successful book-selling company in history—one in which none had hitherto set foot. If Amazon Books is a bridge between the digital and physical worlds of bookselling, then it is one from digital heaven to brick-and-mortar hell—and back again.

To be sure, Amazon Books is less a shrine to its parent company than a showroom for the company itself. A high-profile and high-traffic place where its brand can be seen and the prestige of the company increased. It is more like a billboard for Amazon that one can walk into than a serious and respectable bookstore.

Amazon ate the bookstore, or did you forget? Amazon Books is their mausoleum to the brick-and-mortar bookstore. It is not its savior, nor is it a model for the brick-and-mortar bookstores of the future. If anything, it is a physical reminder that the brick-and-mortar bookstore was killed by Amazon—and is not coming back.

Let's be real. Amazon Books is not a bookstore. It's a creepy corporate showroom.

10

A Class of His Own

How many people can you name that have made major contributions to semiotics, medieval philosophy, and the philosophy of language, in addition to writing a weekly newspaper column and authoring novels that have sold over ten million copies? It's a small club.

Known worldwide for both his philosophical contributions and his best-selling fiction, Italian writer and philosopher Umberto Eco is in a class of his own. His most popular novel, *The Name of the Rose* (1980), which was made into a movie in 1986, directed by Jean-Jacques Annaud and starring Sean Connery, defied expectations about difficult fiction and obscure philosophy by making it popular and fun.

His recent death leaves a vacuum in international letters; there are not many thinkers of his range and stature. Few have been able to blur the lines between fiction and philosophy, the difficult and the popular, as publicly and distinctly as Eco. Of his role as a scholar engaged in public debate, he said, "Journalism is my political duty." It was a duty he performed like few others.

His novels, particularly *The Name of the Rose*, *Foucault's Pendulum* (1988), and *The Island of the Day Before* (1994), contributed to the rise of literary theory in the latter part of the twentieth century. Without these works of fiction, it is hard to believe that semiotics, a major chapter in late twentieth-century literary theory, would have had as much international recognition and intellectual attention as it did, especially in the 1980s and 1990s. Just as Jacques Derrida became the international face of deconstruction during this period, and Richard Rorty the face of pragmatism, Eco, through his academic and popular writing, became the face of semiotics. And a highly visible one at that.

A professor of semiotics at the University of Bologna, Eco came to be associated with the idea that people don't want to be pandered to but rather challenged through writing. "It's only publishers and some journalists who believe that people want simple things," said Eco. "People are tired of simple things. They want to be challenged." And the professor from Europe's oldest university was more than happy to indulge them.

One only needs to look to the sales of his fiction, particularly his first three novels, for ample evidence of his claim that people are tired of simple things. The first one hundred pages of *The Name of the Rose*, for example, are heavy sledding, even for academics. Even so, it has been translated into thirty languages.

Still, to test the notion that "People are tired of simple things," he wrote a novel in plain language that was not overly philosophical or erudite. *The Mysterious Flame of Queen Loana* (2004) turned out to be his worst-selling novel.

But much about Eco defies expectation. Most who write novels as difficult as Eco's do not reach a mass audience. William Gass, for example, took twenty-five years to write his novel *The Tunnel*. It came out in February of 1995, around the same time as Eco's *The Island of the Day Before* (1994). Eco's novel remains in print by its original publisher. Gass's, however, was quickly put out of print by its publisher, Alfred A. Knopf, and if not for being put back in print in 1999 by Dalkey Archive Press would probably still be out of print.

Yet it is not just his success as a novelist that defies expectation, but also how he dealt with it. Most professors who pen bestsellers leave academe as soon as they can to either write more bestsellers or to just enjoy the rewards of fame and fortune. But not Eco.

While his novels sold well enough for him to give up his university position, he refused to, saying, "I am a philosopher." "I write novels only on the weekends."

Also, unlike most professional Anglo-American philosophers who specialize in one area or subarea of philosophy, and work it to death, Eco did the opposite. He was interested in everything. High culture, low culture, and everything in between—and wrote about it all. From James Bond and James Joyce to Marilyn Monroe and Marilyn Chambers, from fake Louis Vuitton handbags and the World Cup to Mad comic books and TV hosts, Eco was not only interested in seemingly every aspect of culture but he also wrote about it for both popular and scholarly audiences. His weekly column, "La Bustina di Minerva," for *L'Espresso* magazine, later collected in volumes with curious titles like *How to Travel with a Salmon and Other Essays* (1994) and *Travels in Hyperreality* (1986) reveal the wide range of his interests. His style of writing in these columns balanced ample humor with considerable erudition.

So, one might ask, how is it possible for anyone to write intelligently and copiously about so many different topics? The answer is to be found in Eco's theory of choice: semiotics. Like one his major influences, the French theorist Roland Barthes, who was also a fine essayist, Eco uses semiotics to produce a seemingly endless stream of interesting statements about art and culture.

One of the leading ideas of Eco's semiotic theory is that the entire semantic universe of the sign-user resembles an encyclopedic labyrinth of meanings, rather than a regulative dictionary of precisely coded correlations. It is within this labyrinth of meanings that disambiguation of the sign occurs, that is to say, within the theoretical frame of intertextuality. It afforded him a bottomless reservoir of material to discuss in both scholarly and popular contexts. This holistic aspect of Eco's work was appealing to many, even to some of his critics such as his contemporary, the American philosopher Richard Rorty.

Eco's early novels hold a unique position in late twentieth-century literature because of the way they seemed to merge semiotic theory with fictional praxis. What makes them even more intriguing is the idea that the formal theory the reader finds in and between the lines is the self-same theory of semiotics that Eco set out in abstract detail in numerous books, articles, and essays.

While many authors have written novels that generate theoretical insights, few have produced theoretical works that rigorously and formally appear to expound the theoretical notions that their novels present. Eco's novels, particularly his early ones, were distinctive in that they were works produced by a major literary and cultural theorist that seem to allude to and assimilate the theorist's own formal insights. And since the publication of his first novel, scores of critics have been debating the very question of how and to what extent his fictions echo his theory.

Some contend that most, if not all, of Eco's major theoretical notions are exemplified through subtexts accessible to the readers of his novels. These general theoretical notions can be found not only in *A Theory of Semiotics* (1976)—one of the most successful formal expositions of this topic and generally considered one of the seminal works in the field—but also other books by him such as *The Role of the Reader* (1979), *Semiotics and the Philosophy of Language* (1984), *Postscript to the Name of the Rose* (1983), and *The Limits of*

Interpretation (1990) as well as numerous other books and articles before and after his entry into the world of fiction-writing. Others, however, challenge a connection between his theory and his fiction.

In *Postscript to the Name of the Rose* (1984), Eco said that one of the aims of an author is to compose texts that compel the reader to "learn something either about the world or about language." His novels arguably achieved both by blending fabulation with semiotic theory. But, as works of metafiction, his novels also perhaps did much more by problematizing the distinction between theory and fiction, laying bare the methods of their own construction, telling their readers how to read them, and self-reflexively examining their own methods of construction. Consequently, they were exemplary contributions to postmodern literature of the late twentieth century.

Eco, in writing metafiction and allegories of reading, belongs in a very strong sense to a genealogy that begins with Jorge Luis Borges and might be thought to culminate with Italo Calvino or even Jacques Derrida. Still, his relationship to this genealogy and its aesthetic is complicated.

In *Interpretation and Overinterpretation* (1992), Eco wrote:

> I understand that, according to a current opinion, I have written some texts that can be labeled as scientific (or academic or theoretical), and some others which can be defined as creative. But I do not believe in such a straightforward distinction. I believe that Aristotle was as creative as Sophocles, and Kant as creative as Goethe. There is not some mysterious ontological difference between these two ways of writing, in spite of many and illustrious "Defenses of Poetry."

His comments recall Mikhail Bakhtin's claim that "After all, the boundaries between fiction and nonfiction, between literature and non-literature and so forth are not laid up in heaven." Still, while Eco wanted to distance himself from the essentialist notion that philosophy and literature are ontologically different, he also wanted to maintain some type of difference. What then, if not ontological, was his "non-straightforward" principle of difference?

Eco wanted us to avoid describing his novels as metafiction, and instead reserve a more traditional fictional designation for them. For him, the decision as to whether a text is fictional or theoretical was to a large degree determined by the writer.

Again, from *Interpretation and Overinterpretation*:

> When I write a theoretical text I try to reach, from a disconnected lump of experiences, a coherent conclusion and I propose this conclusion to my readers. If they do not agree with it, or if I have the impression that they have misinterpreted it, I react by challenging the reader's interpretation. When I write a novel, on the contrary, even though starting (probably) from the lump of experiences, I realize that I am not trying to impose a conclusion: I stage a play of contradictions. It is not that I do not impose a conclusion because there is no conclusion; on the contrary, there are many possible conclusions (frequently each of them being impersonated by one or more different characters). I refrain from imposing a choice between them not because I do not want to choose but because the task of a creative text is to display the contradictory plurality of its conclusions, setting the readers free to choose—or to decide that there is no possible choice. In this sense the creative work is always an Open Work.

Eco is suggesting that we distinguish between fictional texts and theoretical texts on the basis of the conclusion of the text as envisioned by the writer. But doesn't such a maneuver reinstate the value of authorship back into textual criticism? And isn't this what the semiotic criticism which he championed sought to avoid?

Basically, for Eco, any "closed" text that he wrote should be considered a "theoretical" text, whereas any "open text" that he wrote should be considered a "fictional" one. Eco seems to back away from consideration of hybrid forms of textuality such as metafiction, and instead rely on the more traditional distinction between fictional and theoretical texts. Thus, in refusing to describe some of his works as metafiction, he distanced himself from the dominant aesthetic mode of his day. However, by writing works that fit squarely within the metafiction tradition, he seemed to be embracing it.

His self-professed relationship to metafiction is indeed curious—one might even say paradoxical. Eco might have been better off abandoning distinctions such as open work and closed work, fictional text and theoretical text, particularly as they precluded understanding texts such as *The Name of the Rose, Foucault's Pendulum,* and *The Island of the Day Before* as multivalent metafictions. Eco's novels are most significant when they are understood as exemplary of the postmodern aesthetic that dominated the later part of the twentieth century. Doctrines that discourage viewing them in this light should be passed over—even if they are doctrines by Eco himself.

Eco defied expectation, yet again, by asking us to take under consideration the conclusion of the text envisioned by the writer. His foil in *Interpretation and Overinterpretation* was the late-great neo-pragmatist philosopher Richard Rorty, who in part eggs on Eco by saying that having read his theoretical works might give you something *interesting* to say about his novels that you would not have been able to say without having read those theoretical works, nevertheless "it brings you no closer to what is *really* going on in the text than having read Marx, Freud, Matthew Arnold or F. R. Leavis." For Rorty, what is really going on in any novel is a purely contingent matter, and not locatable through the identification of its essential features.

Rorty bolsters his claims with an argument by analogy: just as studying how a word-processing program has been written by the programmer will tell us nothing new about what the program itself can do, understanding the structural logic of a novel will tell us nothing that the literary critic could just gather by reading the novel. "I see the idea that you can learn about 'how the text works' by using semiotics to analyze its operation as like spelling out certain word-processing subroutines in BASIC: you can do it if you want to," comments Rorty, "but it is not clear why, for most of the purposes which motivate literary critics, you should bother." "I distrust," says Rorty, "both the structuralist idea that detecting the presence, or the subversion, of the metaphysical hierarchies is essential."

For Rorty, semiotic theory is merely one model among many that can be utilized to interpret Eco's novels. Moreover, just as you can use a program without knowing its subroutines, so too can you *use* a novel like *Foucault's Pendulum* without knowledge of its theoretical metatext. Each of these supplementary readings, says Rorty, merely gives us "one more context in which to place the text—one more grid you can place on top of it or one more paradigm to which to juxtapose it." "Reading texts is a matter of reading them in light of other texts, people, obsessions, bits of information, or what have you, and then seeing what happens." The value of these "other texts, people, obsessions, bits of information, or what have you" is contingent upon what happens for or to the interpreter when they are used. As such, the rights of interpreters always trump the non-existent rights of texts.

Eco considers the same question posed by Rorty, that is, whether an understanding of his semiotic theory is no more important to a good interpretation of his novels than an understanding of Marx's historical materialism or Freud's psychoanalysis? Why stop here, he wonders? Why not include hermaphrodites,

Herbartian psychology, histopathology, and hydrology to the list as just as reasonable alternatives? Eco's response is simple: because they would deny texts their rights.

Eco says that while it is no doubt true that someone can use a computer program without knowing how it operates or what its subroutines are, it is also true that someone can tinker with a computer program and thereby discover and utilize functions of which the software designer was not aware. Both of these are analogous, in Eco's mind, to the type of textual interpretation that Rorty champions. But what if later on, says Eco,

> comes a good computer scientist who dissects the program, looks at its subroutines and not only explains why it was able to perform a given additional function but also reveals why and how it could do many more things. I ask Rorty why the first activity (to use the program without knowing its subroutines) should be considered more respectable than the second one.

Why is it the case, asks Eco, that an interpretation of the text that describes and explains the "formal reasons that a given text produces a given response" is less respectable than the imposition of random interpretive grids on the text?

Debates such as this one between Eco and Rorty were common in the heyday of high theory in the late twentieth century. Eco adds an important dimension to these debates simply by writing novels during the weekend. Novels that not only teased us to consider their potential connection to his well-established semiotic theory but that also were widely read by people completely uninterested in literary theory and criticism.

Now that we are in the twilight of the questions and issues that drove late twentieth-century fiction and theory, how do we situate the life and work of a Professor of Everything like Umberto Eco? In a class of his own.

—In memory of Umberto Eco (1932–2016)

11

Bootleg Scholarship

Vinyl? Digital? Which music format sounds best? While this debate is never-ending, another is far more accessible but no less difficult to resolve.

Would you rather hear only the officially released songs or get the alternate takes too? What about studio banter and band warm-ups? The official release of a song is often just the tip of the recording iceberg—even for the greatest band of the twentieth-century, *The Beatles*.

"Helter Skelter" ends with a scream from Ringo Starr: "I got blisters on my fingers!" That scream was the result of endless repeats after a long day in the studio. On the eighteenth take, Ringo had had enough. He shouted and threw his sticks across the room. This was the final take and the one that was included on the *White Album*.

There were two "official" versions of "Helter Skelter." The stereo album included the blister shout at the very end of the fade out. The mono version just fades out, no shout. One Beatles song recorded on one September day in 1968 resulted in eighteen takes and two "official" versions.

The story of "Helter Skelter" does not end here. There are more versions of the song recorded by the Fab Four, including a twelve-minute studio version edited down to just over four and released on *Anthology 3*, as well as another studio version that goes on for over twenty-seven minutes. Lots of helter and plenty of skelter.

The cataloging and publishing capabilities of today's music industry allow for more listening, cataloging, and archiving than ever before. For the serious fan and critic, it's no longer enough to just listen to the official release of a song. To gain the proper perspective on an artist, one must consider the outtakes, alternate takes, and smoke breaks. Concert footage on YouTube and bootleg recordings of six nights in SoHo playing the same set list cannot be ignored.

The scholarly record is undergoing a similar evolution. It is a time of great proliferation. In many ways, the journal article and the monograph are akin to the 45-rpm record and the album. However, whereas the music world is convinced that showing musicians' "raw" artistic journey is a positive and uncontroversial development, the scholarly world is not as sure.

Perhaps it is because our data sets and computer models are not as pretty as Dylan's basement tapes? Or because blog postings and discussion boards are on a different level than Springsteen bantering during the *Born to Run* sessions? Or that studying eighteen drafts of a classic essay would even drive the most dedicated scholar to scream like Ringo?

As a scholar in the field of philosophy and literature, I can say with some certainty that if I had the opportunity to see drafts of Borges's stories or hear David Foster Wallace's lectures, I would take it. Such materials are as important to the scholarly record now as the complete Stones sessions from *Exile on Main Street* are to the musical record.

The difference between the case of the musical record and the scholarly record seems not one of quality or quantity, for both records have ample and significant material aside from the "official output." Rather, the difference seems one of economics.

The corporate music industry has determined that there is a market for anything and everything musically associated with its major artists, whereas the academic industry, that is, the neoliberal university, has determined that there is little value in preserving or recognizing academe's scholarly "outtakes." Why?

Because essentially the neoliberal university is not committed to the advancement of knowledge, or even to its dissemination; rather, it is about increasing the bottom line. In no way, shape, or form does expanding the material that counts toward tenure, promotion, and reward from the monograph and the article to scholarly outtakes like blogs and other bootleg scholarship benefit the ends of neoliberal academe.

This of course flies in the face of the realities of how scholarship today *is* produced, namely, to a large extent, through the very bootleg outlets denied recognition by the neoliberal academy. Whether or not these bootleg items should be curated comes down to a cost/benefit analysis.

Does the university spend time and limited resources preserving as part of the scholarly record material that it does not value as indicators of academic performance? Or does it largely ignore the bootleg scholarly record and rely only on the singles and albums—from major labels.

Perhaps the academic industry would be well served by taking a cue from the music industry and valuing more the full range of the scholarly record. Though scholars and scholarship can appear much more vulnerable through the wider window of its outtakes and various types of performance, embracing bootleg scholarship allows us to see scholars and scholarship not just as the products of producers and recording companies, that is to say, editors and publishers, but in more of their academic materiality, which in itself, is more representative of our current critical moment even if it is not in sync with the ends of neoliberal academe.

But if, for whatever reason, the rallying cry for more bootleg scholarship falls upon deaf ears in the academy, all is not lost. For there is still the battle for embracing the proliferation of scholarly records of a more traditional form, namely, scholarship's singles and albums released by independent labels.

There is still a lingering cloud of doubt about articles and monographs released on open access venues. The prejudice is that if the scholarship is not released by a producer with a proven track record of "hits" then the product cannot be of quality.

However, just as you need to listen to a musical record to determine its merit, so too does a manuscript need to be read to determine its academic value. Perhaps pursuing greater acceptance of this evolution in the scholarly record is the most achievable one at the present moment.

The task will not be an easy one, especially considering the social aspects of the current state of open access venues. Much of the scholarly work shared on the internet is wildly unfixed. Articles can be updated or deleted at a moment's notice. Even books published online can be changed, as I realized when the "version" of a book I used in some of my own scholarship "changed" by the time the work hit the proof stage. The situation was further complicated when I found the earlier version to be more profound than the revised publication. What now—quote a book that no longer exists? Not a high point in following the protocols of scholarship.

Alternate takes of scholarly material from the web is one of the more obvious challenges to the stability of the scholarly record. And even though citation through web address and date read denotes that the material was there at one time, it is cold comfort for a scholar who checks sources only to find that they have changed or are no longer there. Nothing is more exasperating for a scholar than discovering that "evidence" has changed or has disappeared.

To say that the scholarly record changes from day to day is not novel. In the pre-digital age, scholarship was produced and published daily. Some of it was preserved in libraries and research centers for posterity, and some was not. However, there is a big difference between preserving a scholarly object on paper and a digital one.

Scholarly digital objects are more than just articles and books. They also include talks and lectures, blog postings, discussion boards, chat rooms, and wiki media. In fact, anything that contributes to an understanding or discussion of a topic of scholarly attention is potentially a part of the scholarly record. In effect, the web as a whole is one the most important elements of the scholarly record. Though given its dynamic nature, "preserving" it is a monumental, if not impossible, task.

Unlike placing a book in a library, placing the web in a repository would involve taking snapshots of it at particular moments in time and storing them. But even if such a "photo" album of the web were possible, it would be like using photos to "capture and store" a baseball game. While the photos will provide a sense of the game, a much more dynamic rendering is needed to capture most, if not all, of the necessary details.

The communal and ever-changing nature of the web is sobering. While preserving or archiving it is impossible, it is still useful for indicating the kind of challenges the scholarly record faces today. The web is one of the most important resources for scholars. However, its dynamism is also one of its greatest challenges for scholars and the scholarly record.

Scholarship needs to be based on evidence that can be verified. If the evidence provided by the web does not lend itself to this form of reliability, it creates a potential weakness in the foundations of scholarship—if not the academy too.

Though we may grimace at the authority of the major producers and pine for independent ones that provide more latitude for alternate visions of scholarship, if we can't access what they are producing because it goes out of print, then what does it mean to produce scholarship related to it? What does it mean when one of the centerpieces of the scholarly record exhibits radical instability and dynamism?

The crisis of authority in scholarship today is more than just what the neoliberal university is willing to acknowledge as legitimate and countable. It also extends to the potential of producing scholarship on a platform with stability and longevity issues. Preserving rotting paper is one thing; referring to scholarship that can simply disappear or change without notice is entirely another thing.

While the social aspects of the scholarly record are one of their most thrilling dimensions, they create a wholly new set of challenges for the academy concerning not only what counts as scholarship but also how it should be conserved. If the article and the book presented by major labels is one of the anchors of neoliberal academe's present, then the dynamic and unfixed world of bootleg scholarship may be more indicative of its future.

In fact, embracing bootleg scholarship may be one of the paths to unmooring us from academic neoliberalism. Inclusion of the immeasurable, the unaccountable, and the unstable elements of bootleg scholarship may be one of the ways out of the value system of neoliberal academe—and into one that values mobile scholarly texts on an equal par with authoritative ones. While the 45s and albums are great, they don't tell the whole story of the scholarly record in the digital age. Finding ways to embrace the evolving scholarly record in its totality may also be part and parcel of the project of moving beyond neoliberal academe.

The scholarly record is evolving and growing now at a faster pace than at any time in history. With so many new ways to contribute to it, it is an exciting time to be a scholar. However, this enthusiasm is tempered by the less than enthusiastic acceptance of the evolving scholarly record by the neoliberal university. Working out the dynamics between the exciting evolution of the scholarly record and the enervating response of neoliberal academe to it may prove to be one of the most important challenges facing higher education today. The "helter skelter" world of bootleg scholarship speaks more to our future than our past.

12

3D Printed Man

Printers aren't what they used to be. Twenty-five years ago, they were essential computer accessories. Today, many regard them as relics from our paper-centric past.

The digital transition and concern over paper consumption's impact on the environment have contributed to a change in use of printers. But printers themselves are changing too.

Printers are not just about paper today. 3D printers can now "print" three-dimensional solid objects from a digital file, which points to dramatic changes in manufacturing and delivery of products. The FDA recently approved a 3D printed prescription pill for commercial use. SPRITAM® could be used by the over 3 million people in the U.S. who suffer from seizures.

And in May of 2013, the world's first gun made on a 3D printer was announced.

The ability of printers to produce *objects*, including guns or drugs, has fostered new fears about them. Whereas before, the greatest fear from a printer was that it run out of toner or ink right at deadline, there are growing fears about potential negative consequences.

When Solid Concepts boasted in September of 2014 about producing the first-ever firearm made of 3D-printed metal that successfully fired 50 rounds, many came to fear for their safety and the safety of others.

A spoof article run in response to the Solid Concepts "event" says it all. The article lead with "A Texas manufacturing company's technological innovation turned tragic on Tuesday when a 3D printer jammed while printing a metal pistol, killing two technicians and injuring an intern."

Soon we'll need safety locks and caps not just for guns and drugs, but the 3D printers that can manufacture them.

But, all joking aside, printers today walk the line between state-of-the-art and old-fashioned technology. Between the increasing obsolescence of one of their oldest products, printed paper, and the amazing emergence of some of their newer products, such as drugs and guns, printers have become a tenacious and adaptable form of technology.

Tenacious because the genealogy of printers can be continuously traced back from the current day to the birth of Chinese woodblock printing circa 600 c.e., a technology that produced whole pages of print. The earliest known printed text dates back to a Buddhist charm scroll that was produced between 704 and 751 c.e., and the first printed newspaper appeared in Beijing, China, in 748 c.e. Moreover, the earliest complete printed book is often regarded as the *Diamond Sutra* printed in 868 c.e.

But for many, the birth of the printer is better situated with the invention of moveable type, a somewhat later invention. Though the Western world likes to claim this invention, it was again the East where it first appeared. Pi Sheng invented moveable type sometime between 1041 and 1048, and the first books to be printed with moveable type were Chinese, sometime around 1050.

In 1440, four hundred years later, Johann Gutenberg and Laruen Janszoon Koster, both of Germany, were the first Westerners to print with moveable type. Gutenberg inaugurated the era of movable type in the West by printing the Bible in Mainz in 1454, and the first book in English was printed twenty years later.

We must also remember that printing is not just important for the mass dissemination of literature and information but also plays a key role in the history of money. For example, the Chinese invented multicolor printing in 1107 mainly to make paper money harder to counterfeit and, in 1806, British engineer Joseph Bramah invented a numerical printing machine for bank notes. To this day, monetary authorities struggle to design paper money that prohibits replication with conventional printer technology.

Flash forward into the nineteenth and twentieth centuries, and the development of printer technology accelerates. The steam printing press was invented in 1814; the rotary printing press, 1847; teletype, 1850; linotype, 1884; monotype, 1887; and offset printing was invented in 1904. Then, in 1938, Chester Carlson invented a dry printing process called "electrophotography," or more commonly termed, "Xerox." Fifteen years later, Remington-Rand developed the first high-speed printer based on the Xerox dry-printing process—an invention that paved the way to a printer (or copier, if you will) known to all as simply the "Xerox machine."

While most of these early to mid-twentieth-century printers will be as unfamiliar to the common person as a 3D printer that can print drugs and guns, the developments since the late 1960s will not be. For this is the period when printers started to become common household objects. Remember the daisy-wheel printer? The dot-matrix printer?

The premier printer, until very recently, was the laser printer. It was developed in November of 1971, when Xerox engineer Gary Starkweather adapted Xerox copier technology for use with a computer. By the mid- to late seventies, high-speed laser printers would start to appear in commercial businesses and, in 1984, HP released the first desktop laser printer. It sold for about $3,500 and was viewed as vastly superior to dot-matrix and daisy-wheel printers.

When I bought my first laser printer in 1990, the price was $500. While it only printed 5 or 6 pages per minute (an eternity), it was worth every penny. No more peeling off tractor tabs! And though HP also released the first mass-market inkjet printer in 1988 for about $1,000, and then offered color in 1994, neither of these inkjets could weather the coffee that eventually ended up on most of my printouts. So laser was the printer of preference of my home office for quite a while.

To be sure, by the mid-'90s, printer technology was on a roll. Prices for units were sinking and the quality of the product was improving. Though the Chinese or Germans might have dibs on the origins of printing, nothing to date could beat having a portable computer provide the instant gratification of a printout.

But soon the unthinkable happened. People started to lose interest in printers in spite of the fact that at no time in history was it cheaper or easier to produce printed items. Word on the street now is that the printer may soon become obsolete.

Really? A technology that can be traced back close to one-and-a-half millennia may just disappear? Well, yes and no.

There will be a growing demand for 3D printers for a long time to come. The technology here will improve and the capacity to produce and reproduce material objects of need and value make 3D printers a good bet into the future.

Saturday Night Live recently[5] played on the high expectations we have for 3D printers in a skit with Matthew McConaughey in the role a 3D printed man. In the skit, McConaughey's 3D man is asked questions along with two other men as part of a tech launch. Though the 3D printed McConaughey somewhat predictably exhibits bugs such as repeating words and giving nonsensical responses to questions, the fact that 3D printing rises to the level of spoof on *SNL* demonstrates how it has captured our imaginations.

However, the same confidence cannot be exhibited in printers that produce and reproduce the printed word and images on paper. Even printers that can reproduce high-quality photos at home are on the wane after a brief period of excitement.

The exception of course is money. As long as there is paper currency, there will be a demand among the nefarious for printers that can faithfully reproduce it. We can do, for example, without more family photos on our desk, especially if they can be stored and retrieved in our computer or mobile device, but the need for money is not obviated by technological progress.

The story of printers today, that revolutionary technology descended from ancient China and Middle Ages Germany, is giving way to another new technology: the iPad. Mobile digital devices make the need to print less urgent. Be they iPad, Kindle, or mobile phone, the notion of having something in addition to the image on the portable screen feels increasingly unnecessary.

When computers sat in dry dock on your desk as they did through the 1980s and most of the 1990s, the need to printout their contents to bring to other locations seemed more necessary. But as the new millennium has unfolded, computing technology has become increasingly more mobile. Data is portable, onscreen.

Take books, for example. Eight years ago, Amazon released the Kindle Reader, a hand-held electronic device that allowed one to store and read books. Nine months after the introduction of Amazon's Kindle Reader, almost a quarter of a million people owned one of the devices. Consequently, demand for ebooks skyrocketed—a demand that increases to this day. In 2008, a year after the introduction of the Kindle Reader, around 63 million ebooks were sold. By 2014, that number ballooned to 512 million. In fact, today it is estimated that almost a third of all new book sales are ebooks.

Around the same time as the Kindle Reader was released, so too was the mother of all printers. In 2007, the Espresso Book Machine (EBM) was introduced at BookExpo America. Advertised worldwide as "an ATM for books," the EBM was about the size of a large office copier and was able to print out a paperback book in just a matter of minutes.

Its developers believed that within three years of its release, there would be at least 500 of these book printers installed worldwide. But time has proven their bold prognostications wrong as roughly only about 60 have been installed worldwide. Though still amazing to see a machine that can print 80 pages a minute and produce a bound volume before your eyes, book technology has moved in a different, more digital, direction.[6]

The failure of the EBM is an important clue to the fate of printers in an increasingly paperless world. But a stronger indication is the story of Hewlett Packard during this same time period. In the fourth quarter of 2008, the largest producer of printers in the world sold more printing hardware and printing supplies that at any other time in their history.

However, the following quarter was much different. The company's sales crashed. From November 2008 through January 2009, Hewlett Packard sales of printers and print supplies decreased by about $1.25 billion, about an 18 percent drop from the preceding quarter. Though there have been some modest increases over the years, figures for the first quarter of 2014, show sales figures just below the sales figures from the first quarter of 2009.

Though HP controls over 50 percent of U.S. market share for printers and printing supplies and 38 percent of global market share, they have been concerned of late that interest in printing is on the decline. One of their concerns is that now many prefer to use mobile devices such as iPhones and iPads to access and read material.

The end of printers, if not also printing, was as unthinkable ten years ago as was the end of books. But technological revolutions and economic collapses can change the world almost overnight. The economic collapse of 2008 coupled with the release of the Kindle and other mobile devices around the same time was a game-changer for printers and printing technology.

Whereas twenty-five years ago a printer that could print out a book would have been revolutionary, today it pales in comparison to the potential of printers that can produces drugs and guns.

A paperless world does not need printers. Or, if it does, they will produce entirely different objects.

Some hope it will be objects like Matthew McConaughey.

13

What's in a Name?

Juliet had a big problem. Her boyfriend had the wrong name. Infamously, she tried to explain it away.

"'Tis but thy name that is my enemy," she said to Romeo. "It is nor hand, nor foot, / Nor arm, nor face, nor any other part / Belonging to a man," continued the Bard's young lover.

The French philosopher Jacques Derrida glosses this line from Juliet as saying that Romeo's name is "inhuman" or "ahuman." "Not only does this name say nothing about you as a totality but it doesn't say anything," writes Derrida, "it doesn't even name a part of you, neither your hand, nor your foot, neither your arm, nor your face, nothing that is human!" Juliet desires that arm, hand, and face, and aims to dissociate her Romeo from his name.

There remains a strong connection—existential, essential, indexical, or whatever—between a person's name and the person. Philosophers such as Plato, John Stuart Mill, and the early Ludwig Wittgenstein describe this connection as a solely denotative one. Others, such as Gottlob Frege, say that proper names both denote and connote, or in Frege's parlance, have a "reference" and a "sense." For him, when names denote they have both a sense and a reference, but when they do not denote, they may have "sense" (connotation) but no "reference" (denotation).

My personal favorite philosophy of proper names comes though from the Princeton philosopher Saul Kripke, who said that proper names are "rigid designators," meaning that they designate the same object in all possible worlds. Kripke even goes so far as to say that a name is attached to its bearer through a baptism of sorts, after which it remains connected to its bearer regardless of any properties that may be attributed to that person. Hence, Nixon is Nixon even in possible worlds where he was not the president of the United States.

Unlike Shakespeare's heroine, who contends that the name of her beloved is something quite different than the young man with whom she is in love, most tend to believe that proper names denote and/or connote *something*. To dissociate a proper name from its object is to deny names their special nature. Names are strongly linked to identity, and are a crucial factor in developing a sense of self and interacting with the world.

"By a name," says Romeo to Juliet, "I know how to tell thee who I am."

The civil rights and women's equality movements taught us to recognize the harmful and hateful legacies spawned by essentializing race and gender. These movements and others were synthesized into the precepts of political correctness that reminded us that regardless of race, class, gender, ethnicity, and sexuality, we need to treat all people equally and not prejudge them based on bias or stereotypes associated with their names.

One of the ways that political correctness regarding "names" was encoded into the humanities was the practice of "blind reviewing." This means that when one submits an article, story, or poem to a journal, it is read by the reviewer without knowing in advance the name and identity of its author. The hope here is that the article, story, or poem is judged on its merit alone, not on the basis of the name and identity of the author.

Or, in Juliet's terms, not on the grounds of an inhuman proper name, but on the human work generated by the bearer of the proper name. Names often lead us to prejudge works; works without names, texts, if you will, help us to avoid evaluation bias.

While some, including literary critic Stanley Fish, disagree with this position, arguing that there is "no merit without bias," most progressive journals today follow the practice of blind reviewing in order to avoid even the perception of bias or favoritism.

Fish argued in favor of bias in peer review because he wanted to reap the benefits that his name brought to his submissions. He worked long and hard at building up his scholarly reputation and having his name on his submissions ensured that all who read them would know that they were his work and not someone else's. You can reject the work of other academics, but you had better think twice about rejecting the work of Stanley Fish.

One of the benefits of knowing the name and identity of the author is that it allows us to read things into the text that may not be readily apparent without knowing the name and identity. For example, knowing an article is by Fish, allows one to read it along with and in the context of his other work. It also allows us to use his identity to help make a decision whether to publish it.

But bias, for many, especially those who aim to be politically correct, is a bad thing. And Fish has made a career of saying the opposite of what the pack says. So it is no surprise that he would argue in favor of bias—when everyone else is arguing against it.

In theory, the system works—until something goes wrong. Namely, the wrong person has their article accepted for publication or, even worse, the right person has their article rejected.

A recent event in the literary world has raised a lot of good questions about bias and its role in the review process. It has also reawakened for a new generation concerns regarding "What is in a name?"

Michael Derrick Hudson wrote a poem called "The Bees, the Flowers, Ancient Tigers, Poseidon, Adam and Eve." A genealogist at the Allen County Public Library, Hudson's poem was rejected by 40 different journals. So the writer from Fort Wayne, Indiana, decided to try submitting it to some journals under the name Yi-Fen Chou, under the premise that a Chinese-sounding name might increase the chances of the poem being published. And he was right.

Of the nine journals to receive Chou's submission, one accepted it. The journal, *Prairie Schooner,* published it in Fall of 2014. Chou's poem was then referred to *Best American Poetry*, where in spite of being rejected by nearly 50 journals (40 as Hudson's poem and 8 as Chou's), Sherman Alexie selected it for inclusion in the 2015 edition.

It was only after Alexie had gone through thousands of poems and selected six dozen for inclusion that he learned that Chou was really Hudson.

According to Alexie, to the extent that he could, he read the *Best American Poetry* submissions blind.

"Each poem will stand or fall on its own merits" was one of his rules for judging the poems. But what do you do when you find out that the author of a poem had a name different from the one on the submission?

Given that one of Alexie's rules was to let "Each poem will stand or fall on its own merits," it would seem hypocritical to deny it publication because the author turned out to have a different name than the one on the submission. To do so would be to acknowledge that in spite of a claim to follow a "blind review" practice, he did peek at the author's name and let it bias his decision.

But, in spite of a "blind review" policy, Alexie acknowledged that he was "more amenable" to selecting the "The Bees" because he thought that the author was Chinese-American.

So, then, the rule is really "Each poem will stand or fall on its own merits *except when the name of the author makes its selection more amenable*"?

In the end, Alexie decided to include the poem in the collection.

"I had to keep that pseudonymous poem in the anthology because it would have been dishonest to do otherwise," wrote Alexie. "If I'd pulled the poem then I would have been denying that I gave the poem special attention because of the poet's pseudonym. If I'd pulled the poem then I would have been denying that I was consciously and deliberately seeking to address past racial, cultural, social, and aesthetic injustices in the poetry world."

The Hudson-Chou affair has been widely and rightly viewed as a fraudulent and racist one. Adopting the name of a Chinese-American in order to appeal to the efforts "to address past racial, cultural, social, and aesthetic injustices in the poetry world" is fraudulent and as racist as blackface performance. There is no way to justify falsifying ones *ethnicity* in order to take advantage of measures to rectify racial, cultural, social, and aesthetic injustices in the poetry world.

However, Alexie's decision to publish the poem, in spite of acknowledging that he violating his "blind review" policy *and* knowing that the author is not Chou, is even more disturbing. The notion of blind reviewing is one intended to eliminate bias in peer reviewing. To have such a policy, yet still allow the alleged ethnicity of the author to temper your decision is as wrong as Hudson's "yellow-face" poetry. Alexie's revelation about how "Chou's" poem was judged taints the entire collection—regardless of the worthiness of the poems included in it.

To judge a poem or article on its merits *regardless* of the race, class, sex, sexuality, disability, and age of its author is the epitome of the meritocratic dream. In many ways, its reliable practice is the extent to which bias and prejudice have become relics of the past. The aim of such a review process *is not* representativeness. *Is not* to address past injustices in the publishing world, rather *it is* to publish what best represents the ideals of the editor, press, and journal.

There is nothing necessarily wrong though with using race, class, sex, sexuality, disability, and age as a criterion for publication, if this policy is openly acknowledged. There is also nothing necessarily wrong with using past publications to inform publication decisions, again, if this is the same policy for all submissions. Decisions to bias or favor particular considerations such as race, class, and gender is always the prerogative of a publication. However, it is wrong to say that one does not consider any of these factors, but to still use them. And worse yet, to use them inconsistently.

The fact that nearly 50 journals rejected a poem does not give one a lot of confidence that it is one of the best poems of the year. In fact, one gets more the sense of the opposite: that the poem is not one of the best of the year and is better left unpublished.

Forty-eight out of 49 editors can't all be wrong.

Still, what's in a name today seems to be more than we want. Blind submission asks us to be like Juliet—and to see names as more representative of our inhumanity than our humanity. But when names *are* used in publication consideration, their denotative aspect strongly links them to persons, personalities, and personas. With one eye we read the submission, and with the other we look over the person. The scales of judgment pivot between a text and a name.

To see publication decisions as linked to our philosophical beliefs about names and naming is to see them properly. The limits of essentializing names and naming have found a new low point in the actions of Hudson-Chou and Alexie. While one understands the desire to get one's poem published or anthology out, there is no excuse for stepping back through names into stereotypes and prejudice in order to do this.

"'Tis but thy name that is my enemy," Alexie might say to Hudson.

"MY enemy, too," Hudson might well reply.

14

Burn This Book

The story of the fight to publish James Joyce's *Ulysses* is remarkable. Outlawed either officially or unofficially in nearly every English-speaking country, the book was confiscated, burned, pirated, and smuggled for many years. Those who printed it, sold it, and distributed it risked going to prison. Even those who carried it through customs could face a $5,000 fine or up to ten years in prison. Yet in spite of these and other risks, many brave individuals contributed to the dissemination of this "dangerous book."

When no publisher would accept it for fear of fine or prison, the owner of a small bookstore in Paris took up the task. Sylvia Beach met James Joyce at a party in July of 1920. Though Beach's bookstore, Shakespeare and Company, had just opened in November of 1919, it quickly became a center and community for literati. The party, hosted by the French poet André Spire, was held to welcome Joyce to Paris, which would become his home for the next twenty years. Beach had not been invited, but was brought to the party by a friend.

Their encounter was fortuitous. The next day, Joyce stopped by Beach's bookstore and began to forge a relationship that would result in her offer in 1921 to publish *Ulysses*. Earlier that year, the "Nausicaa" chapter of *Ulysses*, which had appeared in *The Little Review*, a small journal edited in the states by Margaret Anderson and Jane Heap, was found in violation of New York state law against obscenity. This meant the prospect of publishing the entire novel in the U.S. was slim.

Marked by an obscenity conviction and no viable option for publishing the novel in either the United States or Britain, Joyce vented to Beach. "My book will never come out now," said Joyce. Her reply was simple and direct, "Would you like me to publish *Ulysses*?" The process was far from easy.

The plan was to produce a private edition of the novel sold directly to customers by mail order. Purchasers included Hart Crane, W. B. Yeats, William Carlos Williams, Wallace Stevens, and Winston Churchill. Direct shipping through the mail was illegal, making delivery difficult, but Shakespeare and Company managed to sell twenty-four thousand copies of the book in nine years. By comparison, F. Scott Fitzgerald's *The Great Gatsby* sold nearly that many copies in its first *year* of publication.

Beach's printer, Maurice Darantière of Dijon, did not use a linotype machine to cast the lines of Joyce's six-hundred-page novel. Rather, they were set one letter at a time. Making matters even more difficult was that Joyce was not finished writing the novel even after the manuscript was sent to the printer. He continued to write through the galleys and page proofs, and is said to have gone through as many as four galleys and five page proofs for *every page* of *Ulysses*. Resetting pages of tiny metal blocks was time-consuming and expensive. Fortunately, Beach, with financial support from Miss Weaver, Joyce's patron, allowed him to work with the printer until he was satisfied with each page.

Kevin Birmingham's account in *The Most Dangerous Book: The Battle for James Joyce's* Ulysses[7] of the struggles to bring *Ulysses* to readers is complex and detailed. Though long and meticulously researched, the book is far from tedious. Its twenty-seven chapters are well planned and highly readable.

The characters involved in the battle for *Ulysses* include printers, publishers, anarchists, poets, journal editors, civil servants, wealthy patrons, lawyers, book pirates, and "bookleggers." Each of their stories has been carefully researched, and each is rendered in lucid, entertaining prose with interesting color commentary. By the time the reader reaches Birmingham's fine account of the 1933 obscenity trial of *Ulysses* in the final chapters of the book, jet lag sets in from having gone back and forth across the pond so many times in pursuit of Joyce's story.

Amidst the vast tableau of characters, a few are rendered particularly well. While Birmingham's portrayal of Sylvia Beach and Ezra Pound are credible, they do not shine in the same way as the treatment of lesser-known characters such as Margaret Anderson of *The Little Review*, Pound's friend John Quinn, and most notably Judge John M. Woolsey.

In the case of Woolsey, the judge who oversaw the 1933 obscenity trial of *Ulysses*, Birmingham's research brings him to life so that the reader can almost smell his library and cannot help but admire the remarkable role he played not only in the *Ulysses* trial but also in changing the way obscenity is considered in the legal censorship of books.

Woolsey not only legalized the import of *Ulysses* into the United States but called the book "an amazing tour de force" and described Joyce as "a great artist in words." His ruling on December 7, 1933, that the book "may, therefore, be admitted into the United States" was a victory for Joyce and modern literature, but an even bigger one for corporate publishing. Recall that the reason that *Ulysses* was put on trial was the consequence of a young publisher making sure a copy of it was seized by authorities.

Bennett Cerf, the heir to a tobacco fortune, inherited $125,000 at the age of sixteen. After graduating from Columbia University, he became a successful Wall Street stockbroker and added to his fortune. At twenty-four years of age, he became vice president of the publishing house Boni & Liveright (an achievement facilitated by a $25,000 loan). It was the year after *Ulysses* was first published by Shakespeare and Company, and Cerf now worked for the press that launched the Modern Library in 1917. Horace Liveright tried to acquire Joyce's *Portrait of the Artist as a Young Man* for the Modern Library, but John Quinn said it was too "modern" for the Modern Library. For Quinn, to be in the Modern Library was "a declension into the sunset preceding the dark night of literary extinction."

Nevertheless, Cerf coveted the Modern Library and wanted to own it for himself. In May of 1925, he had his opportunity. Liveright's father-in-law was pushing Horace for payment of monies owed to him. Liveright said to Cerf, "Oh, how I'd like to pay him off and get rid of him." Cerf suggested that an easy way to do this was to sell him the Modern Library. They agreed to $200,000, what Birmingham says was "the highest price every paid for a reprint series." In order to secure the balance of the funds to purchase the Modern Library, Cerf went to his Columbia friend Donald Klopfer. The publishing house that resulted from their collaboration was named "Random House" because they aimed to publish a few books on the side at "random" in addition to the Modern Library backlist titles.

Needless to say, Random House became one of the most powerful publishing houses in the world. In 1965, it was sold for $40 million. While the Modern Library was the cash cow of the press, according to Cerf, its "first really important trade publication" was their publication of the first legal edition of *Ulysses*. Only six years old, the company was looking for a book that would take their press to the next level of success. So, they decided to import a single copy of

Ulysses from Paris and make sure that the government seized it as a violation of the Tariff Act, which banned the importation of obscenity.

Funny enough, the book was not seized at customs and arrived safely at the offices of Random House. Morris Ernst, the lawyer who would defend the book against obscenity charges, took it back to the New York customs office and insisted that they inspect it. When the customs agents saw it was a book that "everybody brings in" and which they don't pay attention to, Ernst demanded that the book be seized.

Judge Woolsey was the perfect judge to try the case. And even though it wasn't an easy case to decide, he believed that "things ought to take their chances in the marketplace." Woolsey's decision opened the door for Cerf's Random House to prosper as the marketplace for *Ulysses* proved substantial. It sold more copies in three months as a Random House publication than it had sold in the preceding twelve years. And Birmingham informs us that after ninety years in print, it sells roughly one hundred thousand copies a year and has been translated into twenty languages.

Birmingham's book shows how Joyce's censorship woes did not begin with *Ulysses* but can be traced back to the publication histories of *Dubliners* and *Portrait*. Among the many heroes in this story are the small magazines that, against threat of legal action and punishment, serialized Joyce's work until the censorship logjam was broken with Judge Woolsey's decision. There are also patrons like Harriet Shaw Weaver, whose total endowment to Joyce was worth more than £1 million in today's currency, and without whom Joyce probably would not have been able to produce his works. Finally, there are friends like Ezra Pound, who fought tirelessly to see that Joyce's work was published.

In fact, there are so many characters, subplots, and stories, major and minor, in this book that Joyce and *Ulysses* sometimes get lost in the dust. But this is never a disservice to wider inquiry. While Birmingham engages and discusses the text of *Ulysses* throughout, he never gets bogged down in it. On the personal life of Joyce, he does a fine job recounting Joyce's relationship with Nora Barnacle Joyce and their children, and the toll of his gradual physical decline. While there is a gruesome account of Joyce having his eye "slit open," Birmingham appropriately limits his coverage of many painful operations and efforts Joyce underwent to save his eyesight.

Joyce comes off in this book as an uncompromising and persistent author who in spite of publisher rejection, legal censure, financial straits, world war, and declining health, was able to compose what is widely regarded as the greatest novel of the twentieth century. From the perspective of an age where anything can be self-published with ease and sent electronically without fear of prosecution, Birmingham's book is a vivid reminder of how far the publishing world has come in such a short time. Less than a century ago, a literary giant could not find a publisher and was the subject of government sanctioned book burnings. Birmingham illustrates well the post office's role in enforcing, if not instigating, obscenity laws of the time.

Birmingham is successful in telling a nuanced story of the publishing troubles faced by James Joyce. *The Most Dangerous Book* is valuable for providing a broad and carefully researched depiction of the events and people associated with the publication—and censorship—of Joyce's masterpiece. In telling Joyce's story, Birmingham picks up the threads of many other stories as well—stories which will be interesting to both students of Joyce and of literary and publishing history.

15

Future Readers

Market niche, target readers, and product promotion are inherent concerns to publishers. Who are the intended readers? How will the book gain its largest reach? Publishers are obsessed with audience.

But what if a book were purposefully withheld from a contemporary audience? What if a group of willing readers were intentionally denied access to a text by their favorite author?

Every text is a time capsule, capturing the thoughts and concerns of writers for preservation across space and time. But what if a work were created specifically to be locked away for years?

Margaret Atwood is the first author to participate in an innovative project conceived by Scottish artist Katie Paterson. Called the "Future Library," Paterson's idea is to ask one hundred authors to write something, anything—a novel, a story, a poem, or even a word—and then shuttle it off into the distant future.

The author is instructed to share it with no one—not even his or her partner or publisher. The writing is to be stored until the year 2114, when the one hundred unknown and unread pieces will be revealed to the public.

One author a year will contribute a piece to Paterson's future library.

Early contributors like Atwood are writing without the benefit (or encumbrance) of reader response. They are writing for a world that may be as different from the present one as ours is from the world one hundred years ago.

One of the fascinating aspects of Paterson's project is that early participants are writing to a future that is very remote and virtually unpredictable. They surely will take a different tone and stance toward the future than later writers.

In the shadow of an unknown century, basic questions like the fate of society and the planet are very much future contingents. Even with just a thirty-some year window, the visionary George Orwell spoke to the tendencies of the titular year of his 1949 novel *1984*, though still overshot them. Imagine now writing for twice or three times that future.

If anyone, Atwood is up to the task.

The collective product of this project will be an amazing document. What did our generation of writers say to the future? A generation caught in the throes of climate change, neo-Darwinian capitalism, technological insurgency, and global unrest? What message did each leave in their bottle?

While the contents of these documents will be unknown, the format in which they will be shared with the public is not.

A forest of one thousand trees have been planted in Norway, which will be felled and used to produce three thousand copies of the hidden library. On the off chance that printing presses no longer exist in one hundred years, one capable of producing three thousand copies of the texts will be preserved along with the manuscripts.

Interested purchasers can buy their set for £600, or about $900. The set comes with a certificate entitling the bearer to a copy of the one hundred texts produced from the pulp of the mature Oslo trees.

In addition, a room in a public library lined with wood from the forest where the trees have been planted will open in a few years in Norway. The room will store the texts of the Future Library, but will not make them public.

There is a certain perversity to a public library that excludes the public until a distant future date.

The holdings of libraries, especially public ones, are by definition transparent and open. Anything within their collection should be available to the public. While some items may go home with library patrons, others are only to be viewed within their walls. Nothing however is off limits, secret, or hidden from public view.

Though library patrons will be able to see the names of the authors contributing to the series and perhaps even the location where their texts are stored, there will be no viewing and definitely no lending privileges extended for items in the Future Library.

Paterson's Future Library is therefore more like a safety-deposit box or vault in a bank than a library item or collection, which is an all too appropriate gesture to publishing in the age of late capitalism. The library's safety-deposit boxes say "private" not "public" property, mirroring precisely one of the key transitional shifts of neoliberal economics. The effect of keeping from the public some of its most precious and unique library contents is to reduce the very notion of a library to that of a bank or holding company. Fine woods and ornate display position the writers and their art further from their adoring readers—and closer to the world of finance and ornate bank lobbies.

To be sure, only writers with tax returns and some level of popularity will be granted the privilege of being held in a "safety-deposit bank" for a century. And it will be their message that we will send in a bottle to the future. But will it be the one that will put our best face forward? Or tell the story of the century? If only popular writers or those with a tax return from book sales are included, will we be short-changing our future audience?

A look to the world of film gives a good image of what it would be like to open up a one-hundred-year-old time capsule to artistic popularity and financial success.

A century ago, the most popular feature film of the year was D. W. Griffith's *The Birth of a Nation*. It was an adaptation of Thomas Dixon Jr.'s novel *The Clansman: An Historical Romance of the Ku Klux Klan*.

What if Griffith, one of the most popular and financially successful filmmakers of his day were asked in 1915 to put his feature in a box that would be opened and played a century later. Imagine that *The Birth of a Nation* were unknown and unviewed by the public until July 2015. Now imagine it being premiered sight unseen to American audiences reeling from racial strife in cities such as Baltimore or Ferguson. Or shown in Columbia, South Carolina, in the wake of its recent confederate flag controversies.

There is no doubt that in these and other contexts the reaction would turn violent, if not deadly.

On the other side of the spectrum, imagine the excitement today when the best-selling novel of 1915, Booth Tarkington's *The Turmoil*, is unveiled to readers a century later. Or, even the second best-selling novel, Winston Churchill's *A Far Country*.

Perhaps not worth a one-hundred-year wait.

The problem with the film and literature that best speaks to the future from the present is that it is often marginal or controversial in its day.

1915 was a great year for literature, but you would never know it from the best-seller list. Major works from that year that most of us would be thrilled to discover a century later include Franz Kafka's *Die Verwandlung* (*The Metamorphosis*), D. H. Lawrence's *The Rainbow*, T. S. Eliot's "The Love Song of J. Alfred Prufrock," and Ryunosuke Akutagawa's "Rashomon." But these works and their authors would never make it into the Future Library in 1915. Why?

Take Lawrence, for example. In 1915, London police seized a thousand copies of *The Rainbow* from the warehouse of his publisher, Methuen, and burned them. The London Daily News called the book "a monotonous wilderness of phallicism." But argue if you want about the worthiness of putting Lawrence, or even Kafka, Eliot, or Akutagawa in a bottle, there is one writer from this time that no one today would want to exclude. Or at least no one who cares about literature.

However, at the time, the greatest writer of his day was unemployed and in debt for two months' salary. A British citizen, he found himself because of the war living in enemy territory with his wife and two children. So, he put up his furniture as collateral and purchased train fare for he and his family to travel from Trieste to neutral Switzerland.

In 1915, James Joyce was about a year into writing his greatest novel—and arguably the greatest novel of the twentieth century. However, he did not have one chapter yet to show for it. *The Egoist* that year had just completed serialization of *A Portrait of the Artist as a Young Man*. But still, compared with Tarkington and Churchill—let alone D. W. Griffith—he was a virtual unknown.

The Egoist, the magazine in which Joyce published his first novel, averaged two hundred copies per issue in sales. If that is not underwhelming enough, consider that it was also just one of the many little magazines published at the time. At the beginning of the century, there were 3,500 little magazines being published with an aggregate circulation of 65 million. From this perspective, the magazine that carried Joyce's voice was but a rowboat amidst the fast speedboats and massive tankers of the little magazine world.

Joyce's problem was not that he was not already a great writer. He was. His problem was that in his own words, "I cannot write without offending people." Thus, from the very beginning, he had difficulty finding publishers for his work. It took him nearly ten years to find a publisher for his story collection, *Dubliners*. Between 1905 and 1914, when the book was finally published, he submitted the book to fifteen publishers eighteen times. But though he prevailed in finding a publisher for the book, in the first six months of 1915, 26 copies of *Dubliners* were sold; in the last six months, only 7. The serialization of *Portrait* in a little magazine was the consequence of his long struggle to find a book publisher for his work.

The point here though is that there is every reason to believe that the authors that we want to speak to the future are probably more like Joyce, Kafka, and Akutagawa in their prime. I'd be embarrassed today to see a forest cut down just to publish unknown works by Booth Tarkington and Winston Churchill.

But more importantly, even if our most worthy writers today *were* captured in the collection, we need them to share their work with us now.

What would twentieth-century *world* literature be without *The Metamorphosis*? Without "Prufrock"? Without "Rashomon"?

Imagine Joyce in this situation, a writer that no one wanted to publish in his day. Who is virtually unread. Who has to go from publisher to publisher, begging to publish a masterpiece. Imagine now someone offering him the opportunity to preserve and protect his work for a century, and then publish it in a fine edition, but deny it an audience in its day.

Do you think he would take up the opportunity to engage an unknown future audience?

Let's hope Paterson's Future Library has the courage to welcome a few adventurous if unpopular contemporary authors in addition to the usual suspects.

16

The Economics of Book Reviews

Book reviews are still one of the more effective ways to garner attention for individual titles. But it is no secret that the rise of the digital publishing world over the past ten years has brought about hard times for the printed book review. Not only have many print venues for book reviews disappeared, it has become increasingly difficult to find financial models for those that remain to persist.

Costs associated with printed book reviews include editing, layout, proofing, printing, mailing, and fees for reviewers. Eliminating printing and mailing reduces the associated costs for these processes, but leaves the editorial, layout, proofing, and reviewer fees. While digital book reviews may be less expensive to *distribute*, they are theoretically not any less expensive to produce.

The economics of books reviews is further complicated by the rapid increase of books published annually each year.

In 2002, around 250,000 books were published in the United States. Ten years later that number increased by nearly tenfold to over 2.35 million books. Moreover, during the same ten-year period, fiction publication doubled. In 2002, approximately 25,000 fiction titles were published in the U.S., whereas ten years later the number would rise to 50,000. It is important to note that this number represents titles released in print format with ISBN numbers. The number would be much greater if one also included nonprint fiction and fiction without an ISBN number.

As the number of books published in the U.S. rises, so too does the competition for book reviews. Nevertheless, the marketing dollars and review opportunities for the vast majority of the new titles published each year is minimal. Only a small fraction of the millions of books published annually will receive promotion beyond a book catalog or online sales listing. There will be no readings at bookstores and displays at trade conferences across the county, and no advertisements in magazines and journals. A smaller fraction still will be reviewed in respected venues that reach a wide audience of potential readers.

The situation for fiction is no different than that for any other publication. Only a fraction of the 50,000 works of fiction noted above are the products of publishers that have the financial resources to market and promote them. Given their special place in the publishing marketplace, these lucky works of fiction require a special name. We'll call them *corporate* fiction.

Not because they are books about corporations or corporate life (that is, the other kind of corporate fiction), but rather because they are the products of companies with immense financial resources that can generate greater interest in and sales of these titles.

Corporate fiction is fiction from a publisher that affords significant resources to marketing and promotion. It is fiction that also comes with a pre-publication advance.

The world of corporate fiction is a special place. The chosen few who enter it are afforded financial considerations and market share for their fiction vastly different from the majority of U.S. writers, a difference made possible through the massive financial gap between U.S. publishers.

Of the estimated 85,000 publishers in the U.S., only about 500 have sales revenues above $50 million. Worldwide, only 50 publishers have sales revenues above $200 million a year, and only 24 exceed $1 billion per year in sales revenue. The most exclusive and powerful group of publishers in the world are the five companies who in 2016 had sales revenue of $4 billion or more.

Sales revenue on the other side of the financial spectrum though is more representative of contemporary publishing in the United States. It has been estimated that in the U.S. alone, there are about 59,000 publishers with annual sales revenues of less than $1 million, and about 47,000 publishers with publishing revenues of less than $50,000.

It is at this point where the economics of book reviews coupled with the relative financial powers of publishers begets one simple truth: *corporate* book reviews are the handmaidens of *corporate* fiction.

Corporate book reviews are in venues that court advertising dollars from corporate publishers by favorably reviewing their titles. They exist both in print and online, though identifying them or proving this relationship can be tricky.

The economy of venues that practice corporate book reviewing is largely hidden. No self-respecting book review venue would ever admit a *quid pro quo* relationship with a publisher. But signs of its existence can be gleaned by focusing not so much on the books reviewed but on the advertisements.

Penguin Random House is the fifth largest book publisher in the world, one of the select few with revenues of over $4 billion a year. They can afford to advertise in any publication in the world.

Book review venues that are on the receiving end of Penguin Random House's advertising dollars are ones that review their titles favorably and have a wide reach and large audience. For these book review venues to distance themselves from the corporate specter they would have to refuse advertising dollars from Penguin Random House, yet still review their titles.

Simply choosing to review titles from the world of corporate publishing does not make a book review venue a corporate one. Dependence on publishers' advertising income, or taking money directly from publishers to review their titles favorably, makes a book review venue a corporate one.

The possibility of a *quid pro quo* relationship between book review venues and corporate publishers is one of the reasons that many regard book reviewing with suspicion. The practice of trading advertising dollars in exchange for positive reviews of titles from the advertised presses diminishes our trust in reviewing regardless of the complicity of the reviewer.

But it is a well-known practice in the world of corporate book reviewing that one selects a reviewer based on their anticipated reaction to the title under review. This of course does not make the reviewer complicit in the corporate book reviewing scam. They are only doing what they were asked to do: review a book. Nonetheless, it is their favorable review that greases the advertising-dollar wheel.

Corporate fiction is fiction produced by big profit publishers, those with the capacity to give million dollar advances and spend similar amounts marketing and promoting individual books. Corporate book review venues are those that have been co-opted in some way by corporate publishers to review their titles.

For some, the worlds of *corporate* fiction and *corporate* book reviewing are simply the worlds of fiction and book reviewing. For others, such as those who run book review venues without considerations of generating profit or the advantage of lucrative advertising deals with corporate publishers, these corporate worlds are not the true worlds of fiction and book reviewing. Nevertheless, to be sure, there are two worlds in publishing and two worlds in book reviewing: one corporate, and the other noncorporate.

American Book Review, the publication that I have edited for past decade, is not, nor has it ever been, a corporate book review venue. Though it occasionally reviews titles from corporate publishers, its focus is on reviewing and discussing writing from small and independent presses—presses far removed from the world of corporate publishing.

Also, it passes the corporate book review "advertising test." A survey of the advertisements included in *American Book Review* reveals a high proportion from the economic underwriter of the review (the University of Houston-Victoria) but none from corporate publishers. It also regularly includes gratis advertising for the various other publications, presses, and organizations housed at the university, including Centro Victoria, Chax Press, Cuineiform Press, *Huizache*, the Society for Critical Exchange, *symplokē*, and others.

For the entirety of its forty-year history, *American Book Review* has been a non-profit publication that takes pride in promoting small press publications. However, when I came on as editor over a decade ago, I noticed that several online organizations were taking the content produced by *American Book Review* and selling it to institutions with little or no financial consequence to the journal.

It was at this point that we came to affiliate with the Johns Hopkins University Press's online division, Project Muse. This affiliation ended the online poaching of *American Book Review* content, and opened up the contents of the journal to thousands of libraries around the world, many of which did not previously subscribe to the journal.

Ten years later, I'm pleased to say that our partnership with Project Muse has been a good one for *American Book Review*. While many of our print book review brethren have died out over past decade, we are thriving both in print and online. This is in large part due to our arrangement with Project Muse; one that gives us a foothold into the online publishing world without diminishing our printed product.

The *American Book Review* is proud to continue its tradition of reviewing publications from presses of all sizes, and grateful for its affiliation with Project Muse.

17

Blurbs in the Post-Truth Era

The endorsements found on book covers, also known as "blurbs," are both a book's most superficial words as well as its most immediately powerful ones. Even before the first line of the book establishes a tone, blurbs have set expectations for the reader.

Are blurbs a necessary service to readers and authors or an unnecessary distraction? Do they enhance the value of books or detract from it? Do they taint our evaluation of books or temper it?

We know that it is unfair to judge a book by its cover, but how many believe the same of blurbs? As a complement to the cover image, book blurbs function as sales pitches. If the goal of publishing is to maximize sales, then books without blurbs are at a competitive disadvantage in the marketplace.

Presses that spurn cover imagery and blurbs set themselves apart from those that embrace them. For example, the mustard-yellow covers with black and yellow print from the Bobbs-Merrill Company's series "The Library of Liberal Arts" were the gold standard of twentieth-century noncommercial publishing.

Aside from the title and author of the book, the price, and the name of the publisher and the series, the front cover of these books only contained a small, simple bird-like icon. The back covers had no text or images. The absence of blurbs on their covers put all of the works in this series on an equal footing. It invited the reader to discover their value by reading them, not by promoting, advertising, or summarizing their contents.

I enjoy a well-designed book cover and I read book blurbs. However, I don't need either if they are intended to oversell a weak book. Moreover, I appreciate and respect the work of presses that carry on the tradition of plain covers with minimal imagery like Univocal of Minneapolis, Minnesota, and Semiotext(e) of South Pasadena, California. Like the Bobb's-Merrill Company of old, they continue the tradition of publishing rich content in simple packaging.

Presses today that avoid cover images and blurbs effectively put all of their books on an equal footing. The Univocals and Semiotext(e)s of the world are essentially saying "Let our titles rise or fall on the basis of what is between their covers, rather than what is on them." There are few better ways to rail against slick corporate publishing than to reject fancy covers and overblown blurbs.

But the radical act of rejecting blurbs and cover images is few and far between in the publishing world. Blurbs are a standard feature of most books published today.

No writer or critic of note dedicates their career solely to writing blurbs. And while book critics are well aware that their comments could end up on a book jacket and many write their commentary to include lines that may serve this purpose, the sole end of critical commentary is seldom *just* the extraction of a blurb. In this way, blurbs are almost singularly unique among the writing vocations.

While poets write poems, essayists write essays, and novelists pen novels, there is no singular vocation dedicated to the blurb.

Blurbs are a parasitic genre of writing. They are parasitic because the power of a blurb is only increased by the name recognition and prestige of the blurb writer *in another genre of writing.*

"If you only read one novel this year, it needs to be Jane Gold's masterpiece *Singular Life.*"

High praise like this is amplified when a literary luminary like Salman Rushdie or Alice Walker is affiliated with the blurb. The same line by a lesser-known writer or left unattributed has much less power. Blurbs require that we know the identity of the source in order to give the statement meaning.

The entire history of this now commonplace practice began in controversy when Walt Whitman decided to share with others a private note from Ralph Waldo Emerson.

Upon the first publication of *Leaves of Grass* in 1855, Whitman sent unsolicited a copy to Emerson, who replied with a note of encouragement. Whitman in turn not only shared Emerson's note with the New York Tribune a few months later, who published it in full, but also put a few words from it on the spine of the second edition the following year. Thus, in gold-leaf lettering on the spine are the words:

I Greet You at the
Beginning of A
Great Career
—R W Emerson

Whitman of course was not the first author to promote his or her book but as far as scholars can determine, he was the first to use the endorsement of a colleague to help sell it—and himself.

Like Emerson's blurb, most blurbs of this type today are brief. Just a line or two. However, no one puts blurbs on the spine any more. The standard rule of thumb in composing them is the more hyperbole the better. But even more so than blurbs that summarize the contents of books, blurbs from other authors are often viewed as highly biased tools of the publishing industry.

Doubts as to their authenticity are compounded when authors brag about writing them without even having read or seen the book. Just as the Sophists gave philosophy a bad name by doing it for hire, authors who only do blurbs for pay give blurbing a bad name—especially when they brag about not having even read the book. There is nothing wrong or shameful in publicly praising work that one admires. But paying our colleagues for praise of our writing crosses a line and stinks just the same whether they've read the book or not.

Those who blurb without good intentions undermine the practice. Knowing that some people write blurbs for pay without reading or caring about the book or author at hand casts doubt on the authenticity of *all blurbs.* Given this practice, how are you to know if a blurb is authentic? Was it written for money or as an uncompensated expression of opinion? Or does this even matter today?

There are of course many authors who do take the time and care to read and think about the work of their colleagues *before* heaping praise on their projects, but it may all be for naught given the bad reputation of some blurbers.

Authenticity and integrity issues aside, blurbs can be considered as a compressed form of criticism or commentary. It is curious then that while few question the authenticity or integrity of the longer form writings of critics and commentators, the same is not true of blurbs.

Criticism seen through the lens of blurbs as its most highly compressed expression is a fundamentally dishonest enterprise, whereas seen through the lens of essays, articles, and monographs is an honest one. How can this be?

Why does one form of criticism fundamentally lack authenticity, whereas the other does not? And isn't it many times the case that the self-same people who write essays, articles, and monographs also write blurbs? And vice versa?

Our problem with blubs may not really be their authenticity or integrity—or even the fact that they are used to advertise and sell books—but rather the way in which they *present* the world of writing and writers.

Book blurbs are inoffensive. Their world is always sunny and beautiful; smart and remarkable. It is one where there are no bad or terrible books. It is a veritable literary utopia.

The praise of our colleagues for our work presents an image of literary solidarity and respect. One where authors value each other and look up to each other. Where they are not egomaniacs looking to squash out their competition in the literary market, but rather one where they unconditionally seek to encourage and celebrate the success of their peers.

If the neoliberal author is an egomaniac who aims to destroy rivals and snuff out competition then book blurbs are a double-edged sword. On the one hand, they are one of the major tools for authors to dominate and corner the literary marketplace—a necessary tool of the neoliberal publishing industry; on the other hand, they work against neoliberal egoism by promoting a vision of literary collaboration and solidarity through their hopelessly optimistic accounts of literary artifacts.

So, even though blurbs *are* superficial sets of words, they are never innocent. And in the hands of corporate publishing, they have become industry tools that further widen the gap between those who can afford to purchase endorsements from the literary elite and those who cannot.

The problem in short with book blurbs is that they cannot be trusted to be truthful. But perhaps in the post-Truth era this is no longer an issue.

18

Starfucker

In the 1960s, rock music revolutionized the music industry. But the change was not immediate, nor was it readily apparent to the industry executives.

When Clive Davis, for example, was made chief operating officer at Columbia Records in 1965, its best-selling music included Broadway soundtracks like *South Pacific*, *My Fair Lady*, and *Camelot*, and artists such as Mitch Miller, who had produced eleven Sing Along albums in a row that went gold. Its roster at the time was limited to Bob Dylan, The Byrds, Simon & Garfunkel, and Paul Revere & The Raiders, who were selling the most of the four. Though Dylan gave the company "prestige," his record sales, says Davis, "were good, rather than great." His only major single at the time was "Like a Rolling Stone." But the times—musically and otherwise—were "a changin'."

For Davis, who had unexpectedly won the "company's executive sweepstakes" and assumed his position at Columbia Records with "no A&R training, no claim to having [musical] 'ears,'" it was the 1967 Monterey International Pop Festival that ushered in "a tidal wave of new music"—one that he would help shape until he was fired from his position in 1973. It was around the same time as this festival, which was held on the Monterey County Fairgrounds in Monterey, California, from June 16 through June 18—and featured the first major American performances of the Jimi Hendrix Experience and The Who—that a young man from just up the road in the Bay area had an idea for a new little magazine.

Drawing its power from its relationship with Dylan's song and a well-known rock band, Jann Wenner founded *Rolling Stone*, a little magazine dedicated to the flowering counter-culture and its music, in the spring of 1967. Only twenty-one years old at the time, Wenner approached the legendary Bay-area music critic Ralph Gleason with the idea. "How about a magazine?" asked

Wenner. "Like the *Melody Maker* and the *Musical Express*, but an American one that would be different and better and would cover not just the records and the music but would cover the whole culture." Gleason thought it was a great idea, and not only offered to write a column for it but to also contribute $1,500 to help get it off the ground.

The first issue of *Rolling Stone* rolled off the presses on October 18, 1967, and featured John Lennon on the cover. Over the next fifty years, it would come to be one of the most influential and profitable magazines in American publishing history. Not only did it establish "rock criticism" as a serious genre but, by many accounts, it "made" what has come to be called "classic rock" music. "The rock stars collective stories, edited by Jann S. Wenner," comments Joe Hagan in *The Life and Times of Jann Wenner and* Rolling Stone *Magazine*, "helped sell millions of records and made them feel good about themselves."[8]

Hagan does a wonderful job telling both the life story of Wenner and the story of the magazine. For some, it will be the biography of Wenner that is appealing, one of an ambitious and ruthless young man who through sheer force of ego builds a company valued in 2006 at $1.1 billion. For others, it will be the story of a magazine that has come to temper the views of many regarding music, politics, and culture for nearly half a century. But Hagan makes a good case that it is difficult to separate the "man" from the "magazine," arguing that *Rolling Stone is* "Wenner's life." Though there were numerous opportunities for him to sell off parts of the company—one whose success was in large part due to the efforts of his wife, Jane—he ultimately refused them all, including an offer to sell the entire company to Hearst in 2006. As Hagan puts it, he "could be a billionaire or he could be Mr. *Rolling Stone*, but he could not be both." Ultimately, he chose to be Mr. *Rolling Stone*, though has now passed along his empire to his son Gus, who studied creative writing at Brown University.

As a business person running a magazine empire (which later would also come to include the lucrative *US* magazine), Wenner is almost without peer in terms of financial success, which he accurately compares to that of Hugh Hefner (*Playboy*, which published its first issue when Hefner was 27) and Henry Luce (*Time*, which he co-founded at the age of 23; *Life*, *Fortune*, *House & Home*, and *Sports Illustrated*). But it should not be forgotten that not only did Wenner have the opportunity to become a billionaire but he also made the record industry a lot of money in the process by promoting the work of particular artists and their music. And, in turn, the record industry supported his magazine. The story here is a complicated one because it took years—and a bit of luck—for the magazine to build up this kind of impact on the industry and its artists.

This dark side of the music industry and the magazine comes out in Hagan's book but not as prominently as it would if the entire volume were an expose on neoliberalism in the music industry. *Rolling Stone* magazine did use data analytics over the years to help determine the content balance that would maximize its readership, something that was important to Wenner from its early days. But once the industry got its hooks into *Rolling Stone*, it went from being the voice of the counterculture to one of the major marketing arms of the music industry.

Perhaps no one of significance in the recording industry has stated more directly the relationship between artistic excellence and profit than Clive Davis in the autobiography he published in 1975, *Clive: Inside the Record Business*, two years after he was fired from Columbia Records:

> Men in the music business . . . are paid to *recognize* talent and then turn this resource into profit. The quest for artistic excellence, and sometimes for showmanship or virtuosity is, bluntly stated, a search for profit. This is somewhat camouflaged by music's emotional lure, its compelling excitement, the industry's glamour, and the challenge of "breaking out" new talent; for these tend to make the business a romantic place. And it is often true that an artist pursues his artistic vision with considerable purity; or an executive can convince himself he's playing a marvelous game and getting paid for it.
>
> Yet any company's accountants, or, in the impersonal world of big business, corporate management, can shock happy executives back to reality in a hurry; they want profits, more and more every year.

If the story told by Davis is one that argues against a romantic view of the music industry, then the one offered by Hagan regarding *Rolling Stone* and its founder is an argument against a similar view of music criticism at its most populous level.

In short, *Sticky Fingers* makes a strong case that in spite of being viewed by its readership as a "serious" forum for rock music criticism through its reporting on "music's emotional lure, its compelling excitement, the industry's glamour, and the challenge of 'breaking out' new talent," all of this and more is ultimately—again borrowing words from Davis—just "camouflage" for its real aim: profit. Wenner achieved profitability for his magazine by joining forces with and befriending industry executives such as Davis, Ahmet Ertegun of Atlantic Records, with whom he co-founded the Rock and Roll Hall of Fame in the 1980s, and David Geffen, who created or co-created Asylum Records in 1970, Geffen Records in 1980, DGC Records in 1990, and DreamWorks SKG in 1994. In fact, in the early years, the magazine "was using Columbia's offices in New York as a virtual bureau of *Rolling Stone*," and had even worked out a deal where "Columbia Records put *Rolling Stone* into record stores through [its] distribution system," which at one time accounted for 15 percent of its single-copy sales of the magazine. Hagan does a fine job in his book relating many of the details of his arrangement with Columbia as well as other industry partnerships.

Much like the book industry in New York, which in the heyday of the print-age pumped large advertising dollars into widely circulated book reviews such as *The New York Times Book Review*, the *New York Review of Books*, and other venues in a relationship that helped their major titles to be featured and positively reviewed by these publications, *Rolling Stone* established a similar relationship with the music industry on both coasts. The magazine benefited by increasing advertising revenue from the industry, while the industry benefited by increased sales through positive and pronounced coverage in the increasingly popular magazine.

But this is only part of the story of *Rolling Stone* magazine and its founder—and perhaps the most banal aspect. Wenner was not just driven to make money, he was also driven to bend the "world to his ego"—and in this aspect, as well as in his "crude egotism, the neediness, the total devotion to celebrity and power," he is much like another person his same age: Donald Trump. Wenner, writes Hagan, "was a pioneer of the age of narcissism. He made his generation feel good about itself—righteous, independent, young. He also hung celebrities like sides of beef in his showroom. The man adored fame." He counted among the "sides of beef in his celebrity showroom" the crème-de-la-crème of the rock world including Mick Jagger, Bono, and Bruce Springsteen. And as Hagan contends, it is often difficult to determine with Wenner where the business ends—and friendship begins.

His longtime "friend," the actor Michael Douglas toasted him a few years ago in front of Al Gore, Springsteen, and others. "So, for years, I thought Jann was just a compassionate, wonderful guy. Rather than a starfucker, you know?"

said Douglas. "And, the reality is," added Douglas over the laughter elicited by his earlier comment, "as we sit here now, in 2006, Jann—he's booked baby, he is booked."

What does it say about a person who is described by a close [movie-star] friend in front of other [celebrity] friends to be a "starfucker"—and who welcomes the description? It says that this aspect of Wenner's personality is not a controversial one: he was obsessed with celebrities and sought out as much interaction with them as possible—and no brackets are needed here. One is a friend of Wenner *because* they are either a movie star or a celebrity, not in spite of it.

From editor of a little counterculture magazine in San Francisco to potential billionaire and admitted starfucker, the criticism Wenner published in his magazine helped make the music industry, especially in late age of vinyl, a lot of money. It also promoted the work of a lot of musicians, many of whom came to be celebrities because of the magazine. But as Hagan's book reveals, Wenner did not build the magazine entirely on his own. Rather, he needed and sought help to do it, and was adept at identifying and surrounded himself with talented employees such as photographer Annie Leibovitz, writer Hunter S. Thompson, and film director Cameron Crowe, who in turn, helped to feed his addiction to celebrity through their artistry.

Though as Hagan insinuates, Wenner's addiction to celebrity has now morphed into *our* addiction with celebrity. "The solar eclipse of Donald Trump signaled the complete triumph of celebrity culture over every aspect of American life," comments Hagan. "A reality-TV star with a casino and a Twitter feed. An egomaniac to rule them all. The message and the medium merged. The message was fame, and fame was money, money was power, and power was just more fame, for ever and ever, amen."

Sad as it may sound, perhaps the final triumph of celebrity culture over American life is that we are all now "starfuckers"—a country so obsessed with celebrity that we elected one as leader of the free world.

Wenner's life is a critical life *par excellance*. His vision launched a genre of music (classic rock) and a genre of criticism (rock criticism). It also made a lot of people rich and famous along the way—including himself. And in doing so, this little magazine went from being a voice for American *counter*-culture to being the culture—albeit one obsessed with celebrity and fame.

For some *Rolling Stone* was a "trade paper." For others, a "critical journal." And for still others, a "teen rag." Wenner's genius though was realizing that it was all of the above—and developing this vision into a media empire and personal fame.

In the end though, after building an empire, and hobnobbing with and befriending American presidents, music and movie celebrities, and the rich and famous, how does Wenner see *himself*?

"I see myself primarily as an editor," says Wenner. "And that's what I have a real skill at." In fact, so much skill that we can and must consider him—egomania and all—among the editorial elite of the vinyl age. Hagan's book does a masterful job surveying fifty years of classic rock journalism and the charismatic, controversial, and crazy editorial genius that was its driving force. It is required reading for fans of rock music—and editors—of which I count myself among both groups.

19

The Fate of the Book

The past ten years have perhaps been the most transformational ones in the history of the book since the invention of the printing press. Electronic books (ebooks) have eclipsed printed books (pbooks) in both sales and popularity; some libraries are now "bookless"; and bookstores are becoming just about as common today as liveries. The single major reason for these changes is the rapid assent of the ebook.

In 1996, Umberto Eco complained in an afterword to Geoffrey Nunberg's landmark collection, *The Future of the Book*, that "[a]fter having spent no more than twelve hours at a computer console, my eyes are like two tennis balls, and I feel the need to sit comfortably down in an armchair and read a newspaper, or maybe a good poem." Around twenty years later, not only are computer consoles becoming antiques, but so too are printed newspapers—and the ones that have survived and thrive do the majority of their business online.

The future of the book radically changed not with the invention of the microcomputer, but with the introduction and development of the e-reader. Specifically, the history of the book changed on November 19, 2007, the day the first "Kindle Readers" were released by Amazon—and sold out in four and a half hours. For it was on this date that many of the major arguments in favor of pbooks over ebooks went out the window.

For one thing, reading material on a Kindle for twelve hours did not leave your eyes like "two tennis balls." While their screens were not as good as the next generation of e-readers such as the iPad, reading ebooks on them left your eyes in no better or worse shape than reading pbooks for twelve hours straight. Their screens were nothing like the "twitchy" little screens found on the computer consoles of the 1980s and '90s, but rather very reader-friendly technologies. In fact, e-readers unlike pbooks allow everything from font size and type to screen contrast and resolution to be adjusted to best meet the individual needs of the reader.

But better screens and different fonts are not the only reason for the rise in popularity of ebooks and e-readers. Portable e-readers now allow one to read wherever one wants, rather than read where one's computer happens to be. One of the best arguments against ebooks was that you could not take them to the beach or curl up in bed with them. Not only can you do this now but you can also annotate the books you read on your e-reader, share favorite passages in them with others, and even determine the analytics of your reading habits.

Nonetheless, a fancy e-reader without the ebooks you want is about as useful as a radio that doesn't get National Public Radio. While it has taken a few years, ebook availability now rivals pbook availability, particularly for new books. Furthermore, many older titles are now available through open access projects such as Google Books. Given all of these developments in the technology of books, book culture is in a period of radical change and transition. Whereas in 1996 Eco could say "It seems to me that computers are diffusing a new form of literacy but are incapable of satisfying all the intellectual needs they are stimulating," the same thing cannot be said today. So, where then does he stand on the future of the book in the new millennium? Sadly, in my estimation, at much the same place he did in the previous one.

Originally published in 2009 in French by Éditions Grasset & Fasquelle as "Ne pensez pas vous débarrasser des livres," Jean-Claude Carrière and Umberto Eco's *This Is Not the End of the Book: A Conversation* is more a homage to the history of the book and book collecting than a statement about the contemporary state of the book.[9] Carrière and Eco's perspective on the book is one wherein the book has persisted since the invention of writing—and has grown to dominance over the long period of the many millennia. If pressed, though, to choose one millennia out of many as the most significant for addressing the declaration offered by the book's title, viz., "This is not the end of the book," they would most likely side with Italo Calvino in the belief that the millennium that just ended was "the millennium of the book, in that it has seen the object we call a book take on the form now familiar to us."

Nevertheless, their perspective on the book is the *longue durée*, not *histoire événementielle* ("eventual history"). Consequently, recent events such as ebook sales eclipsing pbook sales are below their concern—and merely short-range journalistic folly. For a taste of the scope of their point of view, consider, if you will, just a few—and somewhat random—sentences of exchange.

At one point, Eco comments that we are now prey to a new form of censorship. "We can preserve every book in the world, maintain every digital format and every archive," says Eco, "but if some kind of mass crisis suddenly renders untranslatable all the languages we have chosen for the conservation of this massive cultural legacy, then that legacy will be irrevocably lost." Carrière then immediately responds,

> That's what happened with hieroglyphic writing. Theodosius I decreed in 380 [C.E.] that the Christian religion was the single official state religion, and compulsory throughout the Empire. The Egyptian temples were closed, among others. The priests, who were the experts on and depositaries of that writing, found themselves unable to transmit their knowledge. They were forced to bury the gods with whom they had been living for millennia. And along with the gods, their liturgical objects and the language itself. It took only a single generation for all of that to be destroyed. Seemingly for ever [*sic*].

In the space of half a page, Eco and Carrière move from the history of hieroglyphic writing to a possible future where everything in our cultural legacy becomes untranslatable. To add fuel to the fire that it could take a long time to recover our cultural legacy after such a loss, Eco reminds us "[i]t took fourteen centuries for us to rediscover the key to that language"—that is, the language of hieroglyphic writing.

This long perspective on writing and the book is valuable and fascinating—and some of the observations that Carrière and Eco make are simply brilliant. "[T]he book is like the wheel," reflects Eco, "[o]nce invented, it cannot be bettered." But for them, we do not live in a world of ebooks and pbooks, we live in a world where the book is never an electronic object—and always already a non-computer or -technologically mediated one. "Even the mega-gigabyte computer still needs to be plugged in," comments Eco in the same passage. However, he continues, this is "[n]ot a problem with the book"—the pbook, that is. Nevertheless, Eco seems to be unaware that the ebook is not far behind: the Kindle Paperwhite, for example, claims to have a battery life of eight weeks . . . provided that you only use it no more than one half-hour per day.

Both Carrière and Eco are deeply knowledgeable about the history of the book and devoted book collectors. Readers will be awed both by the range of their comments on book history as well as by the depth of their book collections. Still, *This Is Not the End of the Book* feels at times like one is overhearing an incredibly erudite after-dinner conversation between two bibliophiles. And while valuable in itself for the panoramic cultural historical perspective on the book it provides, it would have benefited by the introduction of either another interlocutor with a more contemporary, technophile perspective, or by having a "compiler" who directed the conversation more in this direction.

Carrière and Eco's perspective on the book is more a backward-looking view of the book than a forward-looking one—and this is unfortunate. Even Calvino, who passed away in 1985, long before advances in reading technology such as the iPad, seemed to have more of an awareness of the new book and reading technology era that we have entered than Carrière and Eco. "Perhaps," wrote Calvino in *Six Memos for the Next Millennium* (1988), "it is a sign of our millennium's end that we frequently wonder what will happen to literature and books in the so-called postindustrial era of technology." Unlike Calvino who wonders, Carrière and Eco know: the book will not change.

To me, this is a weakness in their conversation. While it is fascinating to follow an exchange that ranges from St. Ambrose on reading and the Iranian invention of bookbinding to book burning and contemporary book thieves, it is sad how little recognition of the current state of book culture their dialogue offers. While rare and first edition printed books are still very valuable, the value of everyday printed books has plummeted. And these everyday books are the majority of the books that were found in the bookstores that have recently closed—and in the libraries that increasingly refuse to purchase and shelve them.

In some respect, the book space of Carrière and Eco is the rarified one of their personal libraries or collections replete with rare, unusual, and valuable books. From this perspective, books might seem to be like the wheel—and perhaps even more perfect, especially highly desired ones. They allow Carrière and Eco to pursue perfection by building highly personalized collections that serve both their scholarly interests and individual desires. Regarding the latter, Eco comments that he doesn't "show his collection to many people." "A book collection is a solitary, masturbatory kind of phenomenon," writes Eco, "and you don't often come across people who share your passions."

But unlike the wheel, whose perfection transcends time and space, first editions, unusual folios, and book collections are always already in space and time. In one of the more humorous sections, Eco calculates the cost of storing books in his Milan apartment. His conclusion was about 42 euros per book—"[m]ore than the price of the book itself." Moreover, in addition to the space that their collections take up, there is the added notion that these collections do not transcend their owners and cannot be taken with them into death. And it is on this aspect of books that their conversation ends—and reveals the interlocutors at their least decisive.

After hundreds of pages of beautiful reflections on the history of books and bookmaking, Eco and Carrière get tongue-tied and indecisive when they are asked by de Tonnac to comment on the future of their collections. Carrière says his family may "sell all or part of his collection" and Eco that his "collection is so eccentric that I'm not sure whom exactly it would interest." "Perhaps one day," comments Eco, "the real interest in my collection will come from Chinese researchers seeking to understand the follies of the West." But it is with this thought that their "future of the book" thinking really needs to begin.

Eco and Carrière's amazingly wide-ranging and spirited conversation fittingly began with Victor Hugo's famous warning about the book from his novel *The Hunchback of Notre-Dame* (1831) that was set in Paris in 1482. "The book will kill the building," predicted Hugo's Archdeacon Claude Frollo. "When you compare [architecture] to the idea which . . . needs only a sheet of paper, some ink and a pen," continues Frollo, "is it surprising that the human intellect should have deserted architecture for the printing press?"

In a similar spirit, many today believe that digital technology will kill the book—or has already done so. Their reasoning is much like Hugo's comparison of the cathedral to the book: when you compare the printed book to a digital device that can provide access to hundreds of thousands of pages of writing, is it surprising that so many today have deserted the printed page for the digital screen?

Carrière and Eco beg to differ—and have not and will not desert the printed page for its digital double. Their meandering and anecdote-filled conversation on and around this topic will be energizing to bibiliophiles—though nostalgic nonsense to technophiles. While's Hugo's prediction did not exactly come to pass, the invention of the printing press did change the symbolic register of architecture and its "bibles in stone." Most today though seem to follow Frollo's line of thinking when it comes to the impact of Steve Jobs's invention on the book. Namely, that the digital reader will kill the book.

Book collections such as Eco and Carrière's are our Notre-Dames, cathedrals of rare and obscure books constructed by erudite and creative collectors. Each book in their collections is akin to a stone carefully selected to complete a unique bibliocathedral. And like the cathedral, whose value is ultimately found in the building as whole rather than in each stone and windowpane, the individual books in these collections are nowhere as valuable as the collection as a whole, especially one such as Eco's who has become one of the most recognizable writers and critics of our time. The ultimate fate of the book is seen in their response to how their own cathedrals of books will be treated after their death; namely, by destruction and recirculation.

Maybe this is more a comment about the fate of the library than the book. But even so, it reveals that the uniqueness and speciality of the physical book may not be in the individual books themselves, that is, in physical objects widely regarded as digitally replicable. But rather the speciality of the book is found in its coming together in libraries and collections. And that the way we treat them now speaks more to the future of the book than the fate of individual books. This is a scary thought for bibliophiles, particularly given that our book cathedrals (libraries, that is) are slowly goes disappearing in the blue haze of the digital universe.

20

Book Machines

The book world changed drastically a decade ago through two very different machines. One changed the way we read, and the other has aimed to radically alter the book supply chain.

The first machine was a hand-held electronic device that allowed one to store and read books. On November 19, 2007, the first Kindle Readers were released by Amazon—and sold out in four and a half hours.

Over the intervening period, this new technology would revolutionize reading habits and book reproduction expectations, and permanently alter the book industry.

Recall that nine months after the introduction of Amazon's "Kindle Reader," almost a quarter of a million people owned one of the devices. Consequently, demand for ebooks skyrocketed—a demand that increases to this day. In 2008, a year after the introduction of the Kindle Reader, around 63 million ebooks were sold. By 2013 that number had ballooned to 512 million. In fact, today it is estimated that more than 30 percent of all new book sales are ebooks.

As the current dustup with Hachette and the continued growth of ebook sales indicates, Amazon has become a force to be reckoned with in the book industry, especially since this company controls about half of all book sales.

Nevertheless, the release of the e-reader was not the only way that the book world was revolutionized seven years ago. Rather, there was another major announcement around the same time that the Kindle Reader was taking the book world by storm—namely, the release of a portable book production machine.

In 2007, with independent bookstores dizzied by the possibility of people walking around with their entire book collection stored on a hand-held device and worried that the public would no longer need them, the "Espresso Book Machine" (EBM) was introduced at BookExpo America. Widely promoted as "an ATM for books," this so-called "book machine" was about the size of a large office copier with the ability to print out a paperback book in about the time it takes to make a latte.

The 2007 version (1.5) of the EBM was about 8' x 5' and printed about 40 pages per minute. The subsequent model (2.0) was to be even smaller (5' x 4') and faster (80 pages per minute). Initially costing as much as $185,000, but today retailing for less than half of that, $85,000, the book machine was anticipated by its developers to be commonplace in "public and academic libraries, bookstores, coffee shops, university bookstores, university presses, hotels, U.S. post offices and other government offices, reprographic shops, supermarkets, mass retailers, cruise ships, UN agencies, etc."

Manufactured and marketed by On Demand Books LLC, the book machine was touted as promising "to revolutionize book publishing, distribution and sales." Company co-founder and CEO, Dane Neller, former President and CEO of Dean & Deluca (1997–2005), said that he hoped "to have installed over 500 EBM's by the end of 2009."

"Bookstores will be able to reconfigure their floor space to sell faster moving, higher margin inventory and rely on the Espresso for mid- and backlist books," said Neller. "With the EBM no book need ever go out of print, and any book in any language can be available anywhere in the world," continued Neller in a 2007 interview. "More books will be published efficiently i.e., supply will be matched by demand."

The revolutionary rhetoric of the founders was symbolized by their choice of location for the first two public book machine installations. In April of 2006, the previous year, the first beta version of the book machine was installed in the World Bank Infoshop in Washington, D.C. In September of the same year, a second beta machine was installed in The Library of Alexandria, Egypt.

Placing the first machine in the epicenter of the neoliberal economy, the World Bank in D.C., and the other at the site of the allegedly greatest book collection of antiquity, the library of Alexandria, symbolized everything that needed to be known about the machine and its co-founders. They expected the machine to dominate the global book market by enabling anyone with access to it the ability to obtain a hard copy of a large selection of the collected wisdom of the world.

Jason Epstein, chairman of On Demand Books LLC, was the former Editorial Director of Random House, one of the most powerful neoliberal publishing corporations in the world. He was also co-founder of the *New York Review of Books*, one of the great marketing arms of corporate publishing in America, which in October of 2006 contributed to the hagiography of the EBM and Epstein's new business endeavor by publishing an omnibus review by him entitled "Books@Google."

Epstein's account of Google and "the World Wide Web," which "is directly descended from the unprocessed babble transmitted haphazardly by word of mouth and from place to place from which our ancestors forged the wisdom of our species," reads like one big pretentious sales ad for the EBM.

"For millennia this babble had been held in tribal memory, in languages and cultures long forgotten, until the exigencies of burgeoning commerce six thousand years ago—a recent event in the long career of *Homo sapiens*—compelled the invention of written language, the sin qua non of today's documented world including the Web itself," writes Epstein in the first paragraph of his review.

The penultimate major step in this six thousand year history of the collective memory of *Homo sapiens*, for Epstein, however, is Google's "commitment to digitize as many as 20 million public domain titles." A step that provides the sufficient conditions for ultimately the major step: a "machine not much bigger than an ATM which will automatically print, bind, and trim requested titles on demand that are indistinguishable from factory-made books to be read as books have been read for centuries." Namely, not on a digital reader like the Kindle.

"Meanwhile Google," concludes Epstein, "together with the Gutenberg Project and the Open Content Alliance, and similar programs, has turned a new page in the history of civilizations leaving to us the privilege and the burden of carrying the story further." Epstein then closes this book review (or better yet, sales ad) by announcing the EBM installations at the World Bank and the library of Alexandria.

Three years later, on September 17, 2009, Google signed an agreement with On Demand Books that gave them "immediate access to over two million public-domain titles in the Google digital files."

"With the Google inventory," commented Chairman Epstein, "the EBM will make it possible for readers everywhere to have access to millions of digital titles in multiple languages, including rare and out of print public domain titles."

"ODB, in effect an ATM for books," said Epstein upon the occasion of the agreement, "will radically decentralize direct-to-consumer distribution." "Instead of the traditional Gutenberg model of centrally producing, shipping and selling," added CEO Neller, "we sell first, then produce."

In spite of all of the hype and revolutionary rhetoric for this book machine by Epstein and company, it never really captured my attention. Rather, it was and has been the other book world "machine" that was introduced in 2007, the Kindle Reader, that has and continues to fascinate me.

Not because it is not amazing to have access to a machine that can print out a book on demand. But rather because it is more amazing to imagine a machine that can possibly contain within it every book that you ever read or wanted to read—and provide you with direct access to these titles. Call it, if you will, the "Borges Book Machine."

In spite of the grand prognostications of Epstein and Neller, the EBM has come nowhere close to their impact and sales projections for the machine. Whereas Neller anticipated 500 machines installed three years after its release, today there are only 61 EBM machines worldwide. Fifteen of them are in independent bookstores, nine of which are in the United States, three are in Canada, two in the Netherlands, and one in the Philippines. Another sixteen are in libraries, seven of which are in the U.S., three in Canada, three in Egypt (Alexandria), two in the Arab Emirates, and one in the Dominican Republic.

The greatest number, however, are in university bookstores—fifteen in the U.S. and eight in Canada. There is also one in South Africa at the University of Johannesburg, two in chain bookstores in Japan, and one in China (China Publishing Group).

None of them are in coffee shops, hotels, post offices, government offices, reprographic shops, supermarkets, mass retailers, cruise ships, or UN agencies.

Numbers of books reproduced and sold on the EBM is not easily determinable in spite of the fact that all of the machines are powered by EspressNet, "a proprietary and copyrighted software system that connects EBM to a vast network of permissioned content" and "tracks all jobs, and provides payments to publisher."

Still, it is known that Print-on-Demand has recently experienced a steep decline after years of stunning growth.

According to Bowker, one of the main sources of bibliographic information, the nontraditional sector, which consists of reprints (often public domain), other titles printed on demand, and wiki-based material, saw a 46 percent decline in 2013. Whereas 2012 listed 2,042,840 titles in this area, 2013 listed only 1,108,183. This is all the more surprising because the previous year was almost the direct opposite—a 55 percent increase. Namely, the nontraditional sector produced 1,316,714 titles in 2011 compared to 2,042,840 titles the following year.

But the big story in this area of title production is the percentage change from 2002 through 2013, namely an increase of 3,295 percent! In 2002, there were 32,639 titles in this area—an area that remained pretty steady in the five-figure range until the release of the EBM in 2007.

The year preceding the release of the EBM, there were 21,936 titles. However, in 2007, this number shot up to 123,276. By 2009, the number had increased to 1,033,065—and by 2010, bloated to 3,844,278 titles.

The steep drop off in 2011 and 2013 are relatively bad signs by nontraditional title standards. However, by traditional title standards they are still mind-boggling.

In 2002, 215,138 traditional titles were published. Eleven years later (2013) this number has increased by 41 percent to 304,912 titles—slightly down (1.6 percent) from the previous year (2012). But compared to the same eleven-year period in nontraditional publishing, traditional publishing looks flat.

All of this is reason to be excited about what is happening in nontraditional areas such as print-on-demand publishing. However, none of this is not translating into a worldwide proliferation of EBMs.

The one in the Harvard Book Store sits directly opposite the front door of the store. The owner, Jeff Mayersohn, has given it the name "Paige M. Gutenberg." Next to "Paige" is a shelf of "misprinted books" that are selling for $2.00. Mayersohn says that his bookstore sells between 900 and 1,500 direct demand books per month, about half of which are self-published and the other half are reprints. "I consider it as a robust part of our business," says Mayersohn. But not just as a source of direct revenue.

Rather, there is a certain excitement in seeing the book machine for those who have never seen one. "Its still a magnet, a destination for people visiting the store," comments Mayersohn. "If it was too small and much quieter, maybe people wouldn't notice."

In other words, its appeal is more than just utilitarian—more than just its ability to spit out books on demand. It's also a type of entertainment for the curious—one that gets them into the book store, and hopefully loosens their wallets and keeps them interested in coming back.

I trekked across Boston last month to see Paige in action. While the store was packed, no one else seemed much interested in the book behemoth's potential for retail spectacle.

The revolution for this book machine is still in evolution, even if it has now wandered into more of a sideshow or curiosity item than the savior of the printed word.

21

DIY

Self-publishing has always been the underworld of book culture: a haven for esoterica, wild ideas, and half-baked prose. It exists just below the imaginary border between books whose publication is paid by others—and those whose publication is paid by the author.

For many, this border delimits the break between legitimate publishing and its opposite. Just as journals that charge publication fees for articles are often met with suspicion (especially when other journals in the same field do not), so too are books whose publication is fully underwritten by the author, particularly when there are plenty of publishers in the same area that publish books without being paid by their authors—and many of whom even offer them generous advances against their royalties.

More on a par with vanity publishing, self-publishing has long existed as the last stop for authors bent on sharing with the world writing that has been spurned by traditional publishers. For most authors, the decision to self-publish does not involve a choice. Rather, it is a decision of last resort and their only way into the world of published writers.

Until fairly recently, self-publishing was more the exception than the norm in the publishing world. Not everyone has the financial means or the moral will to pay to have their writing published. And historically, even if one had the desire to self-publish, it has always been prohibitively expensive. But the cost of self-publishing has dropped dramatically. Today, it is almost possible to self-publish a book at no cost (provided access to a computer and the appropriate software). Final fulfillment of one of the more egalitarian promises of the digital revolution.

For a little more, one can improve the quality of a self-published book by purchasing various degrees of support. For a slightly higher price, consider a deluxe self-publishing package complete with marketing plans and publicity materials. Exactly how much does all of this cost? Not all that much.

While self-publishing packages can run in excess of $10,000, many are significantly less. For example, for basic ebook formatting and distribution, BookLocker charges authors $675—and only $475 if the author supplies the book's cover. Ebook formatting, conversion, and distribution in this basic package includes the mobi (for Amazon's Kindle) and epub (for Apple's iPad, iPod, and iPhone; Barnes and Noble's Nook; and Kobo) platforms. Also, this basic self-publishing package demands no extra charge to include graphics, tables, or footnotes in printed books—and returning authors are only charged $199 for print setup on their subsequent books (without cover design).

While BookLocker seems to be the lowest priced of the self-publishing companies, many others offer prices that are not far behind. For similar services, Infinity Publishing charges $1,047, Lulu $1,089, CreateSpace $1,151, Llumina Publishing $1,338, Trafford $1,424, iUniverse $1,449, Outskirts Press $1,595, Xlibris $1,673, AuthorHouse $1,799, Dog Ear Publishing $1,998, and Xulon Press $2,396.

These baseline self-publishing packages include a 200-page book with black-and-white interior print formatting, up to 25 interior photos, original color-cover design, print proof, an ISBN for all editions, barcode, a listing on the publisher's website, distribution by Ingram, basic ebook formatting and distribution, and, if you submit your own cover, they will provide you feedback on it. Some also set up an Espresso edition of your book and even give you a couple free print copies.

Need them in a hurry? Production time is within six short weeks. But if you are in an extra hurry, for $999 BookLocker will get your book out in two weeks, which hopefully is longer than it took you to write it.

So, on the low end of the cost spectrum, self-published authors should look to spend in the neighborhood of $600 to $1,200 on a basic print package; up to another $100 for an ebook package; up to $150 for a basic cover design and anywhere from $200 to $1,800 for an advanced cover design. But the costs, of course, do not end here.

If you want a hardcover edition of your book, add about $2,000. For a basic marketing package, think anywhere from $100 to $360. For a press release and author conference appearances, add $1,200 to $3,200. And for the financially secure self-published author, a book promotional video can be had for $5,000.

So, with prices like these, how popular is do-it-yourself publishing? Very.

In 2013, just accounting for the DIY presses listed above, Llumina Publishing published 17 total print and ebooks, BookLocker published 301, Infinity Publishing 365, Dog Ear Publishing 511, Outskirts Press 1,931, Salem Publishing Solutions (formerly Xulon Press) 2,544, Trafford 4,000, iUniverse 4,640, AuthorHouse 11,835, and Xlibris 13,990. However, far outpacing the others in this group are Lulu, which published 74,787 titles in 2013, and CreateSpace, which published a jaw-dropping 186,926 titles.

To be sure, authors are taking advantage of DIY publishing services at unprecedented rates. In fact, self-publishing has now become the fastest-growing dimension of the publishing world to the point where the number of self-published books dwarf traditionally published books.

In 2007, the year the first Kindle Readers were released by Amazon and the first Espresso Book Machine was introduced at BookExpo America, there were 74,997 self-published books published in the United States (or roughly the same number published solely by Lulu in 2013). Of this total, 66,732 were print books, whereas 8,265 were ebooks.

By comparison, in the same year it was reported that there were 407,646 print books published by all publishers including self-publishers. This number is a fairly robust one, though, as it includes all forms of print books including ones that are stapled and laminated. The previous year, when these types of print books were not included, namely, stapled and laminated ones, the figure was 292,353—over 100,000 fewer.

These publication figures are interesting for at least several reasons: first, a broader notion of what is (and is not) a book reveals a significantly higher book output in the United States; second, even as far back as 2007, the dawn of the ebook age, a very high percentage of all books published in the United States were self-published.

Through 2006, figures were not kept on these titles by bibliographic information provider Bowker, the major source for book publishing data. Bowker's data on book output—traditional and nontraditional—is based on ISBN information only. This means that if one does not purchase an ISBN, the book is not included as part of the overall book output data in the United States for that year. There are probably many more books published each year than our standard data set reports.

The shift to a new methodology for Bowker to report annual title output statistics in 2006 is telling—and further confirmation that book culture changed in a very fundamental way in 2007. Not only did the question of what is and is not a book change with the rise of the ebook format around this time, but it also led to a wider accounting of books of all types.

In many ways, new mainstream technologies of the book, such as the introduction of the Kindle and the Espresso, opened the door to a new age of the book. Not only were new forms of publishing becoming mainstream (viz., the ebook), but so too were new forms of printing technology (viz., the Espresso). Now, more than at any time in history, was entry to book publishing more open. But nothing busted open the floodgates of book culture in America more significantly than the rise of self-publishing since 2007.

The year the Kindle and the Espresso were introduced, just about one out of five books published was self-published. However, by 2013 the number would increase by over 600 percent.

In 2013, the number of self-published books published in the United States is reported to be 458,564—an ascent that makes the self-publishing industry arguably the most dynamic and fastest-growing dimension of the publishing industry. It is something which the big five publishing houses quickly learned how to manipulate for their own gain (but more on this next time).

Watch the rise: in 2007 there were about 75,000 self-published titles and in 2008 that number rose by about 10,000. However, in 2009 the number of self-published books increased by over 25,000 titles coming in at 111,359 and in 2010 it increased again by over 41,500 titles over the preceding year. But these figures pale compared to the 2011 data, which reports 246,912 self-published titles—and the 2012 data, which reports a whopping 393,421. The latest data reveals that self-publishing continues to be on the rise with a record 458,564 self-published titles produced in 2013.

To get a context on the self-publishing numbers, consider that in 2012 the number of "traditional" books published was only 309,957—a figure significantly less than the 393,421 self-published titles of the same year.

But the post-2007 self-publishing revolution is only a taste of the more general nontraditional publishing explosion over the same time period.

While the traditional publishing numbers since the launch of the Kindle and Espresso have remained relatively constant, moving from 284,370 titles in 2007 to 309,957 titles in 2012 (a 9 percent increase), the nontraditional numbers have been off the charts.

In 2012, it was reported that 2,042,840 nontraditional titles were published. In addition to stapled and laminated books, these numbers also include reprints (which are often public domain), print-on-demand titles, and wiki-based material. They represent a mind-boggling 1,557 percent increase over the numbers in the same category in 2007. But what is most impressive here is that this increase is not even the high point of the nontraditional area.

In 2008, there were 561,580 nontraditional titles published, but by 2009 this number had bloated to 1,335,474 titles. However, 2010 was the absolute high point for in this year it was reported that there were 308,628 traditional titles published as compared to 3,844,278 nontraditional titles published.

Any way you cut the numbers, traditional publishing is no longer an effective gatekeeper in the publishing world, nor does it represent the majority of books published today. There are many more books published today that may look and feel like products of the traditional publishing world, but are not.

Most DIY books are published with little or no editorial oversight, and at best a modicum of publicity and marketing support. Though they may fulfill the publishing dreams of their authors, their chances of having an impact on the world of literature and ideas—let alone making a profit—is about as likely as their author winning the lottery.

Problem is, many DIY authors do not know this.

The underworld of DIY books is beginning to dwarf the traditional publishing world, presenting a new set of challenges and opportunities for book culture in America. Strange as it may sound, the underworld of DIY publishing is no longer in the shadows of traditional publishing, but is on its way to becoming a serious competitor. The growing giant of nontraditional publishing has become more than just a refuge for bad books, and may very well alter the course of traditional publishing in America.

22

The Boulevard of Broken Dreams

The self-publishing revolution will be televised! Tune in and check it out!

It's the end of gatekeepers warning that a manuscript is not publishable. The end of pesky editors demanding revisions and rewrites. The end of marketing specialists twisting and bending copy to lure in readers and sell books. The world of self-publishing is a writer's dream—a paradise of endless programming on an infinitely expanding number of channels.

Have something to say? Publish it! Nothing to say? Publish that, too!

The self-publishing revolution is equal opportunity and maximally diverse. All voices are afforded a stage; all authors are welcome. While many pay big money to play, any and all can join the revolution with little to no financial obligation. There are many entries into the world of self-publishing, differentiated only by the cost and the size of the dream promised.

But if the self-publishing revolution is televised, it is not on the Big Four (ABC, NBC, CBS, FOX). Nor is it on cable giants like HBO or Showtime or even the public broadcasting mainstay, PBS. In the publishing world, these venues are akin to the Big Houses like Simon & Schuster, Penguin, and Hachette.

DIY publishing is more akin to getting the 4 A.M. slot on your small town cable channel. Sure you get airtime, but you also have to adjust your expectations. Low production value, small audience, and minimal impact are common characteristics, tolerated only by those with no other choices.

Even compared to the smallest of small presses, with a handful of annual releases and a limited or nonexistent marketing presence, most DIY publishing is marginal. Even at their most afflicted, the majority of small presses have an editorial backbone and an aesthetic or ideological *raison d'être*. The same cannot be said of the self-publishing industry, which exists to produce a profit and to prey on the vulnerability of those who desperately want to be published and are willing to do so by any means necessary.

At its worst, the self-publishing revolution is a predatory practice—a financial extension of the neoliberal publishing industry. At its best, it is a revolutionary force that affords a greater diversity of writers and writing to populate the book world.

What then should we make of this revolution in publishing? Should we view it with joy or dismay? Pity or pride?

From the perspective of the thousands of well-run small presses, the self-publishing revolution occurs outside of the gates legitimate publishing. Why? Because at a minimum, a press requires an aesthetic or ideological aim that is guided and promoted by an editor. This minimal condition is a sufficient one to deem some works worthy of the press's catalogue and others unworthy. Without this condition, there is *no* quality control and there really is no *press*—only publishing. Publishing work without consideration of its content is nothing more than mindless duplication. Without an editor's eye, self-publishing is more akin to a mechanical act than an intentional one.

There is something troubling about publishing anything and everything submitted to a publishing house. Perhaps it is found in the very notion of "publishing" itself, a notion that seems to require the interaction of two individuals at minimum: the author and the editor. In a sense, self-publishing is an oxymoron, as it implies a reduction of the author-editor relationship to one of identity rather than difference. Even more radically, one could argue that self-publishing as a practice deconstructs the very notion of publishing by allowing anyone and everyone to reproduce their writing without review.

As the hierarchy of publications shifts and expands to contain everything from peer-reviewed, refereed journals to Wikipedia entries, it becomes increasingly important to trace the source of published materials and the journey they have taken to reach the reader. The responsibility of the reader to understand the provenance of published media grows as the methods of publication expand. The book traditionally has an aura of authority, but the rise in self-published work puts this assumption into question.

The self-publishing industry has become dominant in the publishing world by creating the perception that all publishing is equal—and that all publishers are equal. It plays on the notion that "to publish" is to make one's work available to the "public." While this may be semantically true, it reduces the question of whether or not a piece is for public consumption to a non-issue, when the answer is always "yes."

From the perspective of readers, the self-publishing revolution is either a nightmare or a dream. It is a nightmare if as a reader you do not have the time, energy or will to sort through the half-a-million self-published books coming out each year to choose how to spend your precious and limited reading time. The self-publishing revolution transforms the reading public into editors, as they are forced to sort through works as an editor might. Without the quality control of a press—large or small—the task of the reader in selecting newly published books to read becomes daunting. Some may relish the opportunity to sift through half-a-million books and find a gem. Others turn to curators and advisors from other sources, such as online reviewers or book clubs.

But the process is not unlike rummaging through thrift shops in the hopes of acquiring a Picasso or a First Folio.

The saddest aspect of the self-publishing revolution is not the mountains of junk that are published—presses big and small also contribute to the production of literary waste. Rather, it is the predatory self-publishers who sell authors the dream that publishing with them is hitting the Big Time, promising success on the level of Stephen King and Anne Rice.

The most unscrupulous of the self-publishing services trade on the power and prestige of their parent companies to lure in authors and take their money (and a lot of it).

Simon & Schuster has a self-publishing subsidiary called "Archway Publishing." Established through a partnership with self-publishing giant Author Solutions Inc., Archway Publishing gives their authors a piece of the prestigious publishing house of Simon & Schuster through a number of different packages. The Children's package will cost the self-published Archway author anywhere from $1,599 to $8,499; the Fiction and Non-fiction packages range from $1,999 to $14,999; and the package for Business writers starts at $2,199 and tops out at $24,999.

Operations like this one have all the markers of vanity publishing including the sliding price scale for Business authors—who presumably can pay more than Children's authors—to self-publish their books. How else can you explain the price differential?

Even Harlequin has traded on its name, again through Author Solutions, to form a self-publishing imprint called "Harlequin Horizons." Budding romance writers can now become self-published "Harlequin . . ." authors, albeit for a price. The company promises to include "special services aimed at the romance market, including unique marketing and distribution services."

The biggest controversy in self-publishing, though, is not the shameless selling of publishing brand imprints. Rather it is publishing houses guarding profits in the case a self-published book actually makes it. Though it is as rare as winning the lottery, it can and does happen.

For most self-publishers, once the book is in print, there is no additional financial commitment to the publisher. In other words, if you hit the lottery and sell a lot of copies of your book, then the profits are all yours. But one company decided to do something different.

Launched in April of 2011, Book Country is a self-publishing subsidiary of Penguin. Like the other self-publishers, Book Country charges authors a fee. There are three packages that initially ranged from $99 to $549. The idea is that for a price, authors could upload their self-published work to Amazon through one of three Book Country packages. In turn, the author would have a book listed on Amazon published through a subsidiary of Penguin. While there were complaints about the price of the packages, the real complaints were about the cut Penguin via Book Country would make on Amazon sales.

Normally, Amazon receives a 70 percent royalty on the sale of books directly loaded to their website by authors. While these are loan-shark rates, they are the only option for most self-published authors who want to make their book available for sale to a wide audience. Book Country, however, also took a 30 percent cut of the 30 percent percent cut afforded Amazon to their authors. This mob payment mentality did not go over very well and Book Country has since altered its royalty and payment structure to be more fair to authors for which they have played virtually no role in their success—yet still profit from it.

Packages now range from free to $399, and authors can get 100 percent royalty if they purchase the premium package ($399) and their book is sold through the Book Country retail channel. They report that since 2011, eight Book Country members have sold their books to traditional publishers. Along with the Penguin imprimatur, Book Country is sold to authors as an online writing community. Its policy is that only after one has read and reviewed the work of another member can you then share your work with others. With more than 8,300 active members, they report that each workshopped manuscript receives an average of six reviews.

But this of course is not the dream that DIY authors were sold. Even if we generously view Book Country's eight authors selling their books to "traditional" publishers as success, how then do we regard the thousands of others whose self-published books languish in biblio-oblivion? The self-publishing revolution is in full swing *not* because most of its authors believe that their work will be unread, unsuccessful, low-fidelity productions. Quite the opposite.

It is booming because most of its authors tend to believe that there is no difference between publishing a novel with FSG and iUniverse. But how can that be? Strange as it may sound, for many, the difference between FSG and iUniverse is similar to the difference between Heinz baked beans and the store brand. Though the labels may be different, the products—baked beans—are essentially the same. Both come in cans and both contain beans.

From this perspective, quality is a secondary matter to a more primary material logic: just as all beans are beans, so too are all books books.

Or, if there is a difference between FSG and iUniverse, it is that one will agree to publish your novel and that the other will not; that one sees something in your work and that the other does not. But do people really believe this? Do they really believe that all publishers are equal? Do they believe that a self-publisher who has not read your book really sees something in it? Given the rapid ascent of self-publishing, it appears so. Self-delusion is a powerful force.

But those whose life and livelihood is the printed word know better.

For some, the self-publishing revolution is a victory for the Everyman Author. For centuries, the door to publication has been heavily protected by those whose financial interests and professional reputation could be compromised by publishing not ready for prime-time work. The bouncers at the major publishing houses were kept busy because for every book that the big boys published, hundreds, if not thousands, were rejected. But is publishing all of these rejected titles (and more) really a proud and revolutionary chapter in the publishing world?

To be sure, times have changed in the publishing world, but are they for the better?

We now live in the Age of Acceptance, an age that began around 2007 when the number of self-published titles began to rise significantly each year. With 458,564 self-published titles coming out in 2013 alone—a number that represents the highest annual number of self-published titles in publishing history—one can and should fully expect the numbers to continue to rise. It is not too much of a reach to say that by the time 2015 is all said and done, there will probably be in excess of half-a-million self-published titles that came out over the course of the year.

Again, the best way to consider the impact of these titles on the publishing world is look to the world of television. The impact and significance of 500,000 new self-published titles is akin to 500,000 new channels on your television. And to borrow from Bruce Springsteen's great song from 1992 ("57 Channels"), it's like "Half-a-Million Books (And Nothin' to Read)."

But whereas 57 channels on the television but nothing good to watch is only a quality (or aesthetic) problem, half-a-million books and nothing to read is more than merely a problem of quality—it is also one of ethics.

While some of the DIY publishers sell only the opportunity to publish one's book—with no promise or implication of sales—others take matters a step further. These publishers have come to be known as "hybrid publishers," that is, publishers who straddle the line between traditional publishing and self-publishing. And it is upon them that the highest scorn should be placed.

Hybrid publishing trades on brand recognition to bamboozle authors into thinking that by paying to publish their work with, say, a Penguin affiliate, they are publishing their book with Penguin. In other words, that they are a Penguin author.

This is the metonymic fallacy of neoliberal publishing. Though this fallacy is not limited to the publishing world, using Brands and Branding to lure in desperate authors so that the neoliberal publishers can make a few more bucks is one of its lowest and most predatory instantiations.

If you are so inclined and have a lot of free time on your hands, set your television dial to Channel 500,000 and check out some of the self-publishing revolution programming.

It's on "The Boulevard of Broken Dreams."

23

Welcome to the Machine

Welcome my son, welcome to the machine.

Roger Waters's classic lyrics could serve as words of welcome for new or aspiring writers. Maybe not words of comfort, but few are more appropriate to describe the cold soul of today's publishing world. Hear the synthesized machine sounds played against the lyrics as they are repeated.

In the previous millennium, these words might have been nothing more than a cynical warning to aspiring writers regarding the world of corporate publishing. The rise of neoliberalism in publishing in the latter half of the twentieth century turned the writer's life from an aesthetic endeavor to a market-driven one. This was particularly true of the largest and most powerful global publishing corporations—companies like Random House and Hachette—each with more subsidiary presses than books published annually by the overwhelming majority of the tens of thousands of small presses in America.

Entering the machine of the neoliberal global publishing industry in the twentieth century became less about the dreams of writers than the drone of accountants. It is a machine that has continuously been refined ever since the day Random House sold to RCA. Now that Random House and Penguin have merged—and one in four books sold worldwide is the product of their joint operation—few companies worldwide have a higher global market-share for their product.

Corporate publishing is big business, and growing every year. To enter into it as a new author or aspiring writer is both an honor and a horror. The honor comes with knowing that your writing is part of a lineage that goes back to the great writers of your press. Publishing with Random House, for example, places you in the prestigious company of Sinclair Lewis, William Faulkner, Gertrude Stein, Truman Capote, John O'Hara, and James Joyce.

The honor of being part of an illustrious lineage though quickly gives way to horror *if* the sales of your first book are poor. Don't expect the corporate publisher to wait around five to ten years to see how your book fares over an extended period of time, let alone give you a second chance to publish another with them. Not only are books that don't sell well taken out of print quickly by the big boys, the new emphasis on "pre-sales" as determining the success or failure of your book makes the task even more daunting for the first-time author.

The corporate publishing machine is geared toward low risk and high sales. The handmaiden to corporate publishing is not the perfumed hand of aesthetics or the golden arm of literature, rather it is the calculating brain of the marketing and accounting departments. Big Data drawn not only from sales figures and market analysis but now also individual digital reading habits and social media activity are the key predictors of whether your book will succeed—and when it will fail. The publishing industry today is about providing immediate and maximal gratification to its consumers not testing the limits of literary taste or aesthetic innovation.

The story of the corporate publishing machine is not a new one. Most writers today know the conditions for entry into the market, and are aware at how these conditions have intensified as the machine has grown in size and power. Publishing for Penguin Random House is first and foremost about selling books and making a profit for the global publishing corporation, not about the longevity of *literature*. Who has time to evaluate an author or book's contributions to culture or impact on broader social discussion? Rather, the global publishing machine privileges the immediacy of *fiction*—a world judged solely by balance sheets and units moved.

The safe house for literature is *not* the global publishing machine, especially not the literature that was produced since the last quarter of the twentieth century. Take, for example, one of greatest writers of the twentieth century, William Gaddis. His first novel, *The Recognitions,* was published by Harcourt Brace in 1955, and his second, *J R*, was published in 1975 by Alfred A. Knopf. In 1993, Penguin (now Penguin Random House), reprinted both. However, since 2012, both Gaddis books are now in the hands of Dalkey Archive Press, a small press that will never put them (or any of its catalog) out of print.

But how many Gaddises and Gasses (Dalkey Archive reprinted *The Tunnel,* which was only first published by the global publishing machine in 1995) will be saved from the "out-of-print" death of the machine? And where is the rage against the machine when it comes to its role in the death of literature?

The global corporate publishing machine has the same role McDonald's has in our culture. Everyone complains about its ubiquitous global presence, the way it has put many mom-and-pop restaurants out of business, and diminished our palate—but still billions of burgers are served. And the one in four books served by the penguin company is far greater market penetration than the billions of burgers served by the clown company.

But the global corporate publishing machine taking the likes of Gaddis and Gass off the menu is an especially bad omen for literature today. So where can we look now for a reprieve from the machinations of the global corporate publishing machine? Oddly enough, it may be the very technologies that have opened up book production to the masses, namely, ebook and POD technologies.

If the previous millennium closed with the corporate publishing machine at the apex of its power and control of the global book market, then the new millennium is quickly being defined by the potential of wresting much of this power and control from the accountants—and giving it back to the authors. The unprecedented opportunity today for authors to self-publish their writing provides them with the ability to have absolute control over the products of and profits from their artistry.

The downside of DIY publishing is both that too many *bad* authors are using it as a vehicle to bring to light works that should remain in the dark, *and* that too few *great* writers are using it—an act with the potential to weaken, if not to bring down, the corporate publishing machine. What if Thomas Pynchon, for example, decided to self-publish his novels rather than publish them with Penguin? What would be the effect of high-profile acts of independence from and defiance to corporate publishing? Would such actions spur other great contemporary writers like Don DeLillo to do the same?

While I am not sure that Pynchon's corporate publishing independence day would be widely celebrated by other high-profile and high-profit authors, it is certain that actions like this would be noticed by young and aspiring writers. His assertion of independence from the corporate machine would be a clarion call to the next generation of writers that the future of publishing is with the self-publishing revolution—not the world of corporate publishing.

In the hands of worthy authors, self-publishing can be seen as an act of defiance against the neoliberal corporate world—a world centering upon branding and prestige, not writers and literature. Thomas Pynchon needs the prestige of publishing with Penguin to validate his literary worth about as much as Joyce would need Random House today. Now the financial part of the equation is another matter.

To date, few in the self-publishing arena have been able to produce the kind of profits of publication enjoyed by the big authors at the big houses. Sure, there are writers who have done well self-publishing their work but not along the lines of being able to command six- and seven-figure advances for their work. In the corporate publishing world, solid pre-sales predictions equate to solid advances against sales. In the world of self-publishing, pre-sales figures are about as valuable to authors as buffalo chips.

The publishing machine in the new millennium is very different than that of the old millennium. In the previous millennium, the machine of publishing was an *industry* created around maximally profiting from artistic production. As the industry has evolved, it has come to be dominated by fewer and fewer companies with increasing levels of power, control, and capital. In the new millennium, however, the machine of publishing is quickly becoming a literal one.

Technologies are now available to the public where for a small price, individuals can produce and reproduce on-demand print volumes of the same quality as corporate publishing. Machines like the Espresso Book Machine open up the potential for manuscripts to sit indefinitely in digital purgatory awaiting an audience to find them and print them out. No more relying solely on presses to delimit inventories of titles. Similarly, digital books are a technology that also allows individuals to produce volumes that need never materialize as paper products or warehouse stock. Machines like the Kindle or the iPad open up the potential for ebooks to be downloaded and enjoyed by readers in greater numbers than were ever previously seen by a generation that carted around books in a knapsack.

Since 2007, the year in which the Kindle and the Espresso Book Machine were introduced, the publishing world has enjoyed the rise of a new form of mechanistic existence. In addition, most new and aspiring writers are savvier about opportunities for utilizing these machines for their writerly endeavors than they are with those of the corporate publishing machine. Still, the lure of publishing prestige weighs heavily upon authors. It is seen most exploitatively in the efforts of so-called "hybrid publishing," which draws on the prestige of publishing houses to charge authors a few extra dollars to self-publish their work.

In the new millennium, "welcome to the machine" means something much different to new and aspiring writers than what it meant in the last quarter of the twentieth century. The cold soul of capitalism has finally run the publishing industry into a place that looks more like a dead end than the road to the future. Gone are most of the bookstores and the print-review venues that were in the pockets of the publishing industry. What remains is a digital expanse that offers anyone and everyone the opportunity to not only self-publish reviews but also to easily and affordably self-publish books.

Within this brave new digital world of publishing is the opportunity to rage against the machine of corporate publishing by embracing technologies for book production and reproduction that are outside of their control. The question is whether writers will use this opportunity to produce and disseminate important, innovative, and aesthetically challenging literary work or whether it will be more of the same. Hybrid publishing is a step back to the future of corporate publishing; self-publishing though is a step into a future where writers are in full control of their work and any benefits that they may produce.

My hope is that our welcome to the new machines of publishing is one where the aesthetic, social, and political dreams of writers are provided with absolute freedom and autonomy from corporate censure and control. Welcoming new and aspiring writers to the machine is to welcome them to the opportunity to find an audience for their work. Corporate publishing aimed to manufacture the needs of its audiences, whereas self-publishing gives the power of aesthetic choice back to the reader. If some of the great writers from our generation were to embrace the opportunity to self-publish their work, there is even more reason to believe that the publishing world of the future will be more progressive and democratic than the publishing world of the past.

Welcome to the new machine of the publishing world.

24

Crisis? What Crisis?

Higher education in America is in crisis—or is it?

If the pages of the *Chronicle of Higher Education* are a worthy barometer of our "crises," then we are indubitably "in crisis." According to their search engine, there are over 6,000 articles on the *Chronicle's* website dealing with our various crises, with the "debt crisis" and the "humanities crisis" topping the list with about 725 articles on each topic. But is the proliferation of higher-ed "crisis" journalism because we are truly in "crisis" or because "crisis rhetoric" sells papers?

Perhaps a false dilemma, but still a fair question to ask because for the academic barker, few terms are as effective in attracting our attention as "crisis." Though other rhetorically supercharged terms such as "birth" and "death," "new" and "old," garner our attention and are commonplaces of academic journalism, nothing seems to get our blood boiling faster than the use of the term "crisis" in association with anything higher ed. Or, perhaps, is it that nothing raises our anxiety level more than identifying our "crises"?

Some psychologist or narratologist can probably explain the attraction of crises better than I can. All I know is that everywhere I turn today in the house of higher education all I hear about are our crises. Tenure, debt, funding, job, and humanities top the list of high-profile higher-ed crises but I'm sure that with your help the list would expand.

Still, shouldn't we be asking whether all of these things really are "crises"—or whether they are something else? Perhaps I'm throwing in the crisis towel too fast, but aren't we just a little fast and loose with this term or does 6,000 articles in one journal alone dealing with higher ed's crises seem reasonable to you?

It might very well be argued that the rhetoric of academic barkers regularly features the noun "crisis" in its depictions of higher education not to announce a crucial or decisive point or situation but simply to voice displeasure with the ongoing state and direction of higher education. Many times a situation dubbed a "crisis" is less a "turning point" than a standing and stable condition, albeit an unliked or unfortunate one. But calling a standing state of affairs "unfortunate" or "unliked" does not have the rhetorical weight or darkness of "crisis"—does not instill terror in the academic heart anything like designating it a "crisis." A series of "unfortunate situations" warrants a drink, whereas a series of "crises" tells us it's time to get drunk.

Maybe I'm being too sensitive to the power of words and am old-fashioned when it comes to semantics, but dubbing something a "crisis" indicates that it is truly a "turning point." Having your home burn down and losing all of your earthly possessions is a "crisis." More students choosing to major in business rather than the humanities over the past decade is unfortunate, but not a crisis. There are worse majors and at least these folks are in college—which is half the educational battle anyway.

If, however, this turnabout in business versus humanities majors occurred suddenly and unexpectedly, then we might consider it a crisis. But when the turnabout is the result of a gradual transformation in undergraduate major selection, it does not warrant the crisis appellation. In fact, from the perspective of our colleagues in the business school, calling it a crisis is an affront to their academic integrity. The humanities might be dubbed "in crisis" if at some point in the near past they were one way, but now they are another way—and the new way is unliked. It makes no sense however to say that they are in "crisis" when in point of fact they have been in their current situation for a decade or more. To call them in crisis under such conditions is irresponsible—or worse.

So, the temporal focalization of crisis is important. If philosophy departments are now closing at a higher rate than they are opening, and this is a relatively recent phenomena, then we can responsibly call this a crisis, particularly if we are philosophers or think that the study of philosophy is an essential or important part of higher education. It is a crucial point in the history of departments of philosophy when they begin to decrease in number. Usually it means that they have reached a peak and are beginning to fall off. But as a crisis or turning point, it cannot be a continuing condition of higher education and still be dubbed a "crisis." Crisis does not mean continuing condition. It implies a turning point such that after a period of time it just becomes the state of things.

This is not a trivial or irrelevant distinction. To say that higher education is in crisis because of the rise of neoliberalism is for all intents and purposes a misnomer. Neoliberalism has been at work at least since that 1980s and its direct impact on higher education has been ongoing for at least the past twenty-five years. Though there have been periods of intensification, strictly speaking, higher education is beyond the point where it is in "crisis" because of the ascent of neoliberalism. Same with student debt and the job market. Each of these was at some point in the past indeed a "crisis," but now they are merely the continuing condition of higher education in America.

I'm not suggesting that any of these former "crises" are situations that we should like or be happy with or even accept. I am, however, suggesting that to dub them "crises" is not only a misnomer but at this point in academic history, irresponsible. The train has left the station. We are a debt society; we live in the age of neoliberal academe; the job market for PhDs is weak—and getter weaker; academic freedom *is* under assault; etc. All of these things are the case—but they are not crises. But why we continue to call them "crises" as opposed to working to move beyond them is the question of the day.

My own belief is that higher education deteriorated beneath the feet of many of us—and for one reason or another we were powerless to stop it. Using the rhetoric of crisis allows us to assume a level of plausible deniability for the deterioration. It allows us to voice our displeasure with changing aspects of the academic world. But, a humanist who has worked for twenty-five years or more in higher education and who declares that there is a "crisis" in the humanities is only calling attention to their own failings.

The humanities failed to become what they had hoped they would become and thus by dubbing them now in "crisis" are saying that forces beyond their own control brought them to their current condition. Can you think of one humanities professor who says, "You know, if I had only taught my courses differently, we might not be in this situation." Or, "If we ran our department differently, then we could have avoided the current state of affairs?" No, it is always everyone else's fault that the humanities are failing, never our own.

The rhetoric of crisis is the last refuge for those who wish for an academic world different from the one in which we currently live. It is the term that both relieves them from any responsibility for the situation in which we are in as well as says to the world that I don't like things the way they are—and want them to go back to a former state of affairs. The reality however is that the world has changed around them—and that they are not ready to accept it.

I've fallen into the crisis trap a few times myself but now always try to reserve the use of it for true turning points versus complaints about our situation. There is no crisis of neoliberal academe; rather, neoliberal academe is the condition from which we need to move beyond. We need to try to actualize academic worlds wherein we are not merely the docile subjects of neoliberal managerialism. But this will take acts of resistance and visionary performance. This is why I have suggested that we take up a more combative rhetoric in these times of education through the looking glass.

Instead of dialogue, I prefer paralogy. As a model for critical exchange about the university "in a time of crisis," it encourages views that destablilize and disrupt a system of education that from most accounts is beyond repair. Paralogy's agonistic dimension facilitates speech about the university that is passionate even frenzied. It calls for academics to become emotionally involved in university dialogue and encourages tough metaprofessional criticism. It is a rhetoric of "struggle" and "conflict" against a massive and repressive vision of the university—a guerrilla war of the marginals.

In short, a dialogical approach to the university that aims at consensus and stability within the existing system is not going to solve its problems—or bring about the downfall of the neoliberal university. Reform and change in higher education moves at a glacial pace—a pace at which one cannot reasonably hope to solve the educational systems' problems before the system as a whole collapses. This is why a paralogical approach is preferable in this time of systemic crisis.

I'm probably in the minority with not being enamored by the rhetoric of crisis, but whether you agree with my assessment or not, I ask that you consider that there must be a point where we stop complaining about the conditions of higher ed and bemoaning a past that is no longer recuperable, and begin to live in the present. I wager than once you stop thinking about our academic condition as a crisis, you will begin to open up a space to regard it as one in which transformative and progressive action can reshape it into one which is more to your liking. Perhaps the solution is to truly create a crisis—a turning point—rather than to simply point them out—and paralogy has that power to do this.

25

How to Be a Critic

Few major critics today are as comfortable being critical as Marjorie Perloff, and there is no better place to see her dishing out her unique appraisals than this wonderful new collection of interviews and essays.

In *Poetics in a New Key,* Perloff reminds us of the value of honest, direct assessment: "I have many colleagues who never dare to say what they think, especially in a public situation," comments Perloff. "But we need a little courage!"[10]

"Never in my own lifetime, I feel," she laments, "has 'poetry' been quite as badly written as it is today; never have there been so many 'poets' who are literally talentless and yet win all sorts of prizes and awards and get professorships in good universities."

Never one to mince words, Perloff is at her critical and cantankerous best in this new book that collects interviews and essays first published between 1997 and 2012.

"In reading earlier criticism," says Perloff, "it's interesting to see how vicious people could be: John Hollander could just dismiss "Howl," or the Lowell camp could dismiss O'Hara with impunity." "But now," she continues, "everyone is so polite."

Well, maybe not everyone.

Perloff recalls the "After the Flood" conference, where she was the only woman on a program that included Harold Bloom, W. S. Merwin, John Hollander, and Richard Howard. Perloff read a paper on the performative poetics of John Cage and David Antin.

When she finished there was silence, ultimately broken by Harold Bloom who demanded, "Do you think these writers are of interest to anyone? I don't think people here need their time wasted by discourse about such writers."

One of Perloff's students raised his hand to ask, "Professor Bloom, don't you think it is time to move into the twentieth century and open yourself up to new things?"

Bloom was livid. "Young man you have insulted me!" he replied, standing and exiting the stage.

Though Bloom publicly apologized to Perloff the next day, his apology was no less controversial. "I must apologize to Marjorie for yesterday," said Bloom, "because it was like three men . . . raping one woman!"

Perloff comments that this was one of "the best things that ever happened to me, because if I could deal with this barrage of direct insult, I suppose I could deal with almost anything."

But what makes Perloff's own brand of harsh criticism so powerful is that she does not just administer critical remarks to others, but also turns it upon her own work. This critical self-reflection is an admirable quality—and *Poetics in a New Key* showcases excellent examples.

In an interview with New York University professor of English Peter Nicholls, she weighs in on the greatness of the literary innovators she so eloquently championed in *Unoriginal Genius* (2010), including Charles Bernstein, Susan Howe, Kenneth Goldsmith, and Toko Tawada.

"Do I think the poets I discuss in Unoriginal Genius," asks Perloff, "can match the great Modernists—say, Yeats and Eliot, Pound and Stein? Certainly not—not even Ashbery, I'd say, can match them."

It is this intense dialectics between reverence and disdain for critics and poets of the past and present that makes reading Perloff's work so energizing. With her, good guys become bad guys—and bad guys good. Take, for example, her relationship with the work of Ezra Pound and Charles Olson.

She explains that while in graduate school at Catholic University, many of her professors and classmates visited Pound, who was institutionalized for eleven years at St. Elizabeth's Hospital in downtown Washington. Perloff, however, went in a different direction.

"I never quite wanted to participate in these visits, disliking, as I did, the poet's politics, his displays of racism and anti-Semitism." Nevertheless, after reading some of Pound's essays, including "A Retrospect," she "was hooked."

On the other hand, Perloff has deep reservations about the writing of Olson—a writer widely admired by her colleagues. "I myself, for example, have never shared my colleagues' admiration for Charles Olson; for me he fails on two counts: his language does not have the density I look for in poetry, and his rhetoric is insistently and overtly masculinist in ways I find irritating." This comment comes from the Preface of *Poetics in a New Key*, written in December of 2013. However, her dislike of Olson's work may be traced back in *Poetics* to an essay she published about him in 1973.

"Charles Olson, as I argued in an essay called "Olson and the 'Inferior Predecessors'" in *ELH* in 1973 or so—an essay I never reprinted in book form because it made people so mad but also convinced a lot of others of the case—took most of his "Projective Verse" essay straight from Pound and [William Carlos] Williams." "I demonstrate the 'steals' in a long list," continues Perloff in this 2006 interview with Jeffrey Side. "Olson had little original poetics, but he did try to expand Pound's internationalism so as to make it less Eurocentric or Chinese-Japanese-centric."

Nonetheless, after forty years of unfavorable regard for Olson's work, Perloff is still open to being convinced otherwise. "Make a good case for Olson," says Perloff, "and I am quite willing to back down—at least to a point." "[T]his is why I am so drawn to the conversational mode of the interview," continues Perloff, "—I am quite willing to be persuaded that I have been wrong."

This too is why the fourteen interviews in the collection make for such inspiring reading. Perloff is a gracious interlocutor with all interviewers, including those who seem unaware of her pioneering and vast contributions to the field.

If Perloff is right, and "a slightly exaggerated, controversial view forces people to think," this book is nothing if not thought-provoking.

Some representative Perloff agitations:

"Poetry reviews," writes Perloff, "are mostly just puffs." "One would think each poet reviewed were a genius!"

"What do you think of cultural studies?" asks an interviewer. "I think it has done incredible harm," responds Perloff.

"Continental philosophy from Derrida onwards doesn't really help much, because in many ways," comments Perloff, "Derrida was doing exactly what the poets had already done." "[I] have increasingly come to feel that the mystification endemic in Deconstruction was a dead end."

And so on.

Following the currents and counter-currents in this book is a thrilling ride. No position or person is beyond reproach; and nothing is off the table when it comes to literary studies.

"There is no progress when it comes to the literary field," says Perloff, "there's only *difference.*" Or does she mean "différance"? You never know with her—and she seems to like it that way.

Poetics in a New Key is an excellent introduction to the critical genius of Marjorie Perloff and her dictum that "language has to resonate." "The words have to, so to speak, explode in your face." This reviewer urges caution when reading *Poetics in a New Key*—a book whose resonance tends toward the volatile, with most expertly overseen explosions.

26

The End of Book Country

What happened to book country? To the many bookshops in cities large and small awaiting eager customers? To an American landscape dotted with bookstores large and small from coast to coast? What happened to the invisible pathways though cities like Chicago and New York where one could pass through neighborhoods by traversing a series of wonderfully unique bookshops? To places where serendipitous readers young and old could get lost for hours hunting through shelves in search of unexpected treasures?

Book country is slowly disappearing. As bookshops dwindle in number, the paths through book country become fewer and more arduous. No longer should one expect each town or neighborhood to have a bookshop. No longer should one expect to relive memories of a place by seeking out old book haunts—rather, one should expect only ghosts of our bookstore past.

A decade ago, many independent bookstores were sent into extinction by the corporate book chains. Now, even the corporate bookstores are but a shadow existence of what they were ten years ago.

It is sad day when one gets nostalgic about the era of cookie-cutter corporate bookstores such as Borders Books or Barnes & Noble, but such is the time in which we live.

In the Los Angeles area alone, Acres of Books, Barnes & Noble Westside, Barnes & Noble Encino, Barnes & Noble Woodland Hills, Bodhi Tree, Bookie Joint, Borders Books, Cliff's Books, Cook's Library, Dawson's Books, A Different Light, Dutton's Beverly Hills, Dutton's Brentwood Books, Dutton's North Hollywood, Equator Books, Heritage Book Shop, Latitude 33, Metropolis Books, Midnight Special, Mystery Bookstore, Mysteries to Die For, Portrait of a Bookstore, Samuel French (Valley), Village Books, Williams' Book Store, and Wilshire Books have all shut their doors in the past ten years.

And for LA bibliophiles, this list does not even include favorites such as the Pickwick Bookshop and Hunter's Books that closed more than ten years ago.

For many, there is no substitute for a brick-and-mortar bookstore. Shopping for books online does not compare to the bookstore experience. This is particularly true of a bookstore whose character and stock is as distinct as the style of a great writer—or even a great publisher. What has become of the temples of the book world? One need only glimpse to midtown Manhattan for an answer.

The Charles Scribner's Sons Building on 597 Fifth Avenue in New York City was designed by the prominent American architect Ernest Flagg. Constructed in 1912–13, the building is a ten-story Beaux-Arts, limestone-fronted temple to one of the most celebrated publishers in American history. The elegant iron shop front with a vaulted interior adorned with delicate ornamentation was designed to resemble a small library. The Scribner Building is as grand as the many classic American authors that fill its catalog, and the illustrious customers who browsed its shelves.

The Scribner Building is from a different age—the golden age of American publishing. A century later, it stands as a physical reminder of how far publishing and bookstores have changed. We tend to present our products as we value them (consider the sleek, refined glass structures of the Apple stores), and the thought of a contemporary store built with the reverence for space and books of the Scribner building is hard to imagine.

The Scribner Building has given way to the needs of the new millennium. No longer a grand store for the great publishing company, it is now occupied by a popular beauty products retailer.

Customer Jay Friend was on hand as the Scribner Book Store was nearing its last days in January 1989. *New York Times* reporter David Dunlap recorded Mr. Friend's thoughts: "When I grew up, there were two great Fifth Avenue bookstores—Brentano's and Scribners. . . . They were both magical places, but Scribners was even more so. It was like a library. When you walked into Scribners, you felt a certain reverence."

"Places like this," he said, "will never be replaced."

Both the interior and exterior of the Scribner building have been landmarked by the New York City Landmarks Preservation Commission, and a plaque explains the history of the building. While the books may be gone, the setting is preserved and ripe for the imagination. However, the vast majority of our bookstores, grand and pedestrian, have simply been reconverted to other uses, abandoned, or torn down. There are no signs or plaques, no recognition of their past uses or history. They simply disappear.

At their grandest, bookstores were not just places to purchase books but sites designed to inspire our intellect and engage our curiosity. At their most pedestrian, bookstores were simply places where those seeking truth and beauty could convene with others with similar passions. And unlike libraries, which allowed us to borrow and return knowledge, bookstores held out the promise of making that knowledge a permanent part of our lives through acquisition.

What has changed is not the promise of truth and beauty from books, but rather the necessity of filling our lives with their physical presence. A beautiful book by a writer who we admire used to be an acquisition that added value to our lives. It was something that we sought not just for what was contained between the covers but also because of how the physical object signified our intellectual and aesthetic values.

Today, bookstores are being read their last rites. Their treasures are now either virtually available in e-reader format or stored in a central warehouse in the Arizona desert to be retrieved by robots and presumably soon to be delivered by drone. A far cry from the personal attention and service of the bibliophiles in the opulent interior of Scribner's.

So, what's left? What are the remains of book country, particularly after the chains and online retailers decimated the independents?

To be sure, the majority of book purchases today are done online—and at an increasing rate. In 2013, combined online sales revenue of pbooks and ebooks was 7.54 billion, whereas sales of pbooks in brick-and-mortar stores amounted to only 7.12 billion. Also, many more people are choosing ebooks over pbooks, with current estimates that more than 30 percent of all new book sales today are ebooks. In 2008, around 63 million ebooks were sold, whereas by 2013 the number has ballooned to 512 million. But the chains too are dying—even the smaller ones.

Just over twenty years ago, there were 3,293 chain bookstores in the United States. Leading the list were Barnes & Noble with 1,343 stores, followed by Waldenbooks with 1,268. Far from the top were Crown Books (257), Zondervan Bookstores (126), and Bookland Stores (101). Further back were Encore Books (65), Lauriat's (48), Cokesbury (40), and Kroch's & Brentano's (19). At the bottom were Tower Books and Borders with 13 stores each.

Twenty some year later, Barnes & Noble had roughly the same number of stores, but only Cokesbury, which is owned by the United Methodist Church and is a self-supporting nonprofit, remained from the 1991 chain outlet list—and with a few more stores (57). The rest were gone, including Borders, whose rise and fall over the intervening period has been well documented.

In addition to Barnes & Noble and Cokesbury, the 2011 list of chains included Family Christian Stores (283), Books-A-Million (232), Hastings Entertainment (146), and Half Price Books (113), for a total of 2,206 stores.

In the summer of 2014, this group took another large hit when Hastings Entertainment was bought out for $21.4 million. At its peak, the franchise had 154 stores branching from Washington state and Idaho down through Oklahoma and Texas. Today, however, there are 126 stores left. While not as large or dominant a franchise as Barnes & Noble or Borders, it still has stores in 19 states.

Founded in Amarillo, Texas, in 1968 as a retailer of books and music, Hastings has struggled of late like all of the chains. While in 2006 it had $548 million in revenue, by 2012 it was down to 463 million. Books amounted to 22 percent of their revenue in 2012, about 101 million, with video also amounting to another 22 percent. A workforce of 7,000 employees was reduced to 2,000. In response to the digital downturn for sellers of books and music, Hastings tried to reinvent itself by emphasizing the sale of products more profitable than books and music, namely, action figures, comics, movies, games, electronics, sports items, novelty gifts, hobby items, and apparel. But even this was not working—there are only so many action figures one can buy.

Hastings has been sold to Draw Another Circle, a Delaware company formed by Joel Weinshanker, president and sole shareholder of National Entertainment Collectibles Association, based in New Jersey. Weinshanker's company controls the merchandising and licensing rights for Marilyn Monroe, Muhammad Ali, and Elvis Presley and operates the Graceland tourist attraction, and was a major supplier of entertainment collectibles to Hastings.

You should not judge a book by its cover. But does the same hold true for book*stores*? Should you judge them by the covers in their front window? By their displays? By the racks of Metallica t-shirts and bobble-head Star Wars figurines?

It is no secret that the bookstore is going the way of the record shop. But is it really better for them to survive as the last stop for Elvis and Skywalker memorabilia—or to just fold up and become a historical memory?

Book country in America is now more like the gift shop at Graceland than the vaulted ceilings of Scribner's.

It has become a bad country song—that is nearing its end.

27

There Is No Success Like Failure

Pete Seeger was furious.

It has been said that upon first hearing the sounds of the amplified instruments, Seeger had "turned a bright purple and begun kicking his feet and flailing his arms."

People around him that afternoon feared what action the co-writer of "The Hammer Song" might take. One person who saw Seeger's reaction commented that they had never seen a trace of violence in Seeger, except at that moment.

He threatened to shut off the electricity, but cooler heads prevailed—the audience was agitated and shutting off the electric could easily have escalated the scene into a riot.

Fortunately, Seeger didn't have a hammer at the time, or he might have used it on the brash young singer-songwriter from the Midwest.

On the evening of Sunday, July 25, 1965, Bob Dylan opened his set at the Newport Folk Festival with an electric version of "Maggie's Farm."

The times, they were a-changin'.

Seeger passed away in 2014, and his reaction to Dylan at Newport in 1965 was mentioned as often in remembrances as his prodigious musical accomplishments. While the artist who upset him had only released his first album a few years earlier (*Bob Dylan*, released March 1962), Seeger's career had almost two decades on Dylan's. In the 1940s, Seeger was widely heard on national radio and, in the 1950s, he had a string of hit songs with the musical group the Weavers. Why get so worked up about a young upstart musician plugging in at Newport?

Dylan's band was not the only one at the 1965 festival to use amplified instruments; the Chambers Brothers and the Paul Butterfield Blues Band were also electrified. In fact, the Butterfield Band, which performed earlier than Dylan at the festival, was given an ovation by the Newport audience. Muddy Waters rocked the festival with an electric set the previous year at Newport. So what was it about Dylan's set that turned Seeger's face purple?

Like Woodie Guthrie, Seeger was known and celebrated for his protest music. Songs like "The Hammer Song (If I Had a Hammer)," co-written with Lee Hays of the Weavers, and "Turn! Turn! Turn!," which he adapted from Ecclesiastes came to prominence as hit songs in the sixties through covers by popular groups such as Peter, Paul & Mary ("Hammer" [1962]) and the Byrds ("Turn!" [1965]).

His songs were also covered in the sixties by Trini Lopez, Joan Baez, the Kingston Trio—and even the star of *The Blue Angel* (1930), Marlene Dietrich.

By the sixties, he was one of the most publicly prominent and well-known singers of protest music in support of civil rights, international disarmament, and environmental protection.

His popularization of the spiritual "We Shall Overcome" became an anthem for the civil rights movement—one that school children all over the country at the time sang for their parents in assemblies as a sign of solidarity.

For many in the audience that day, he represented the folk music establishment.

However, as Seeger knew and sang so well, "to everything there is a season."

The summer of 1965 was just one year removed from the summer of 1964, the so-called Freedom Summer. In June of 1964, thousands of out-of-state volunteers, along with thousands of black Mississippians, set out to register African American residents of the state. At the time, Mississippi had the lowest percentage of African Americans registered to vote in the country (6.7 percent in 1962). Ninety-percent of the out-of-state volunteers were white and most of them were from the North.

There were many in Mississippi who resented "outsiders" interfering with their affairs. Freedom Summer was a violent one. Though the entire registration project in Mississippi only lasted ten weeks, it resulted in 1,062 arrests of out-of-state volunteers and locals, 37 church bombings and burnings, 30 black homes or businesses bombed or burned, 80 Freedom Summer workers beaten,

4 civil rights workers killed, and at least 3 Mississippi blacks murdered because of their support for the Civil Rights Movement.

In the new book *My Mantelpiece: A Memoir of Survival and Social Justice* (Why Not Books, 2014), Carol Goodman, the mother of Andrew Goodman, one of the three civil rights activists murdered by the Ku Klux Klan on June 21, 1964, recalls her conversation with her son about participating in Freedom Summer. "He wanted to be a beacon of light in the heart of darkness," says the young man's mother. "How could I deny him?" Though torn between protecting her son from harm and allowing him to fight for what he believed in, she "permitted him to go to Mississippi because that is who he was." "And," comments Goodman, "it is who I was too."

Fifty years ago, social activism in America was much more dangerous than it is today. While the voter registration movement still rages on, especially in states like Texas with high Hispanic populations, American citizens don't lose their lives fighting for civil rights as they did in the heart of the sixties half a century ago. Goodman comments that there are "40 names inscribed on the Civil Rights Memorial in Montgomery, Alabama. Of the 40 victims, 19 were killed in Mississippi. One of them is my son. I allowed him to go there, and I was both guilt-ridden and proud." One of the legacies of the sixties is a greater tolerance for social justice and actions that forward it.

Many of the artists and writers from the sixties (like Seeger, Dylan, and Joan Baez) stood toe to toe with activists in the pursuit of social justice and civil rights. Nevertheless, fifty years later we can look back on Freedom Summer as both a success and a failure.

A failure because of the many lives that were damaged and destroyed as a result of simply trying to ensure that all citizens of this country were registered to vote. Carol Goodman says that in spite of the ambition of the Mississippi Summer Project, which would also form "'freedom schools' to teach African-Americans about their constitutional rights" in addition to the voter registration drive, "many people involved with the project, we learned later, secretly believed that the violence these so-called Yankee do-gooders would incite would direct the nation's attention to the intolerable conditions in the state." "It was a recipe," comments the murdered young man's mother, "for martyrdom."

This was summer in America fifty years ago. It was also a summer where Muddy Waters, an African American musician, played without incident an electric set to a predominantly white audience at a musical festival in Rhode Island.

A year later, four African American brothers from Carthage, Mississippi, performed an electric set at the same festival without incident, though to some excitement. Guitarist Joe Chambers recalls that the audience at the Newport Folk Festival in 1965 were breaking down fences and rushing the stage. "Newport had never seen or heard anything like that," said Chambers. When their set was over and the crowd finally settled down, the MC said to the audience, "Whether you know it or not, that was rock n roll." Their set also motivated their bass player, George Chambers, to start playing an electric Danelectro bass rather than a washtub bass.

Come gather round people wherever you roam.

On the evening of July 25, 1965, Bob Dylan played three electric songs and two acoustic ones in a set between those of two traditional folk groups, Cousin Emmy and the Sea Island singers.

Dylan did not bring a band with him to the festival, but decided spontaneously that he needed one. He organized a pickup band comprising three members of the Butterfield Band (guitar, bass, drums) along with pianist Barry Goldberg. They practiced until dawn the night before their performance.

The hostility began as soon as Dylan, dressed in leather with an orange shirt, laid into "Maggie's Farm." The crowd booed him and called him a "sell out" and told him to play "folk music." The heckling continued through "Rolling Stone" and "It Takes a Train to Cry." After the group left the stage, however, there was a long silence.

Peter Yarrow convinced Dylan to go back on stage with only his acoustic. At the request of the crowd, he played "Tambourine Man" and closed his Newport performance with "It's All Over Now, Baby Blue."

There has been much speculation as to why Dylan went electric that night. While Seeger represented the folk music establishment, Dylan was its promise and future. The most obvious reason for the shift to electric was aesthetic independence. Dylan was announcing a new musical aesthetic in much the same way Igor Stravinsky had done fifty years earlier at the premiere of his "The Rite of Spring." On May 29, 1913, Stravinsky's Paris audience was sent into a frenzy by Stravinsky's score and Nijinsky's choreography. And just like Dylan, he was booed during the performance. Carl Van Vechten later said that many in the audience that night thought that Stravinsky's piece "was a blasphemous attempt to destroy music as an art." So too thought many in Dylan's audience.

But, in spite of the negative audience reactions, neither Stravinsky nor Dylan were attempting to destroy music. Rather, both were trying to *restore* music as an art. Moreover, historical distance reveals both to have been successful—in spite of the public failure of their marquee performances.

For, as a wise man once said, "Failure's no success at all."

A new dialectic between success and failure is at the heart of the Freedom Summer and Newport '65. And fittingly, no one has described its complexity better or more succinctly than the man from the North country.

In his 1965 classic, "Love Minus Zero/No Limit," Dylan captured well this new attitude, with the line ". . . there's no success like failure/And failure's no success at all."

With this line—and his performance at Newport '65—Dylan announced a change in attitude toward commercial success and artistic failure. It is an attitude that arguably carries on through today.

Writing thirty years ago, novelist and editor Ron Sukenick commented well on the dialectic between success and failure. "Through the forties and the fifties artists pretended to have standards totally separate from that of the commercial culture, standards which, however, tended to crumble at the first sign of success," wrote Sukenick. "Warhol, Mailer, Seymour Krim and Norman Podhoretz did a good job—maybe too good—of demystifying the arty cult of failure. Artists of all kinds now frankly acknowledge the power of commercial criteria. We have caromed away from the cult of failure back once again to the good old American cult of success. The question has become whether there remain any criteria to the practice of the various arts, or whether standards are determined totally by the market place. It is only artists who can answer this question because they are the ones who best know their arts."

These questions opened up by the artists of the sixties still haunt us fifty years later. To be sure, the neoliberal arts establishment is predicated upon the notion that commercial sales equate with aesthetic success—and that artistic failure is tantamount to commercial failure. But Dylan showed us another way. A way that embraces aesthetic failure as the engine for commercial success and social justice.

"We don't need validation by the market place," continued Sukenick in the same piece. "We award recognition on our own terms."

Sukenick's comment is still apropos. The digital age has made it much easier to recognize and validate work that is a commercial failure though an aesthetic success. Today there are far fewer barriers to artistic distribution and critical recognition as anyone with access to the internet can make their artwork and criticism available to an increasingly digitized public.

Theoretically, this also makes it easier to utilize the arts as a means to support social justice and democratic values, in particular, the ones that Seeger, Dylan, Baez, and other prominent artists of the sixties fought so hard to bring to the awareness of an increasingly socially progressive nation.

In many ways, our continuing embrace of failure as success is one of the most enduring legacies of the sixties.

Clearly, there's no success like failure.

28

Hardback Justice

New Jersey governor Chris Christie made national news when his staff was linked to deliberately producing traffic congestion on the George Washington Bridge. Staff members were purportedly sending a message to some of Christie's political adversaries who had not been supportive of the Garden State governor's reelection campaign.

Impeding the free flow of public travel between New Jersey and New York City is one of the lower forms of political revenge. Waiting in snarled traffic for hours burdens not only the governor's detractors but also his allies and just about everyone else. The only group that seemed to benefit from this act of retributive justice was the Christie team itself. But even that changed once investigation of the guilty parties commenced.

Acts of retributive justice such as this one are difficult to justify ethically. While the Christie team obviously saw some "justice" in punishing the "wrongdoing" of their political adversaries through manufactured traffic congestion, most people don't see it see this way, particularly those leaning on their horns stuck in traffic for hours.

What if the manufactured traffic congestion had been virtual rather than actual? What if it was snarled traffic not on a vehicular highway but rather on a virtual one? What if it were one of the most traveled superhighways in the world?

The founder and CEO of Amazon, Jeff Bezos, made international news when his staff deliberately produced e-commerce delays on Amazon.com. Amazon, which is said to control about 50 percent of all physical and electronic book sales, has been delaying shipments and refusing pre-orders for titles by publishing giant Hachette. Taking a page out of the New Jersey political playbook, Amazon is playing hardball with Hachette Book Group over ebook profits. In short, Amazon wants a bigger cut of Hachette's ebook profits and is willing to inconvenience Amazon customers and punish Hachette authors in order to leverage a deal would allow Amazon to retail Hachette books at prices below their competitors.

From Amazon's perspective, slowing Hachette traffic on the e-commerce superhighway has distributive justice on its side as the public will benefit from the lower prices at which his company can offer their books.

"When we negotiate with suppliers, we are doing so on behalf of customers," said Amazon. "Negotiating for acceptable terms is an essential business practice that is critical to keeping service and value high for customers in the medium and long term."

No wrongdoing here, just good old hardback capitalism, says Amazon. "Negotiating with suppliers for equitable terms and making stocking and assortment decisions based on those terms is one of a bookseller's, or any retailer's, most important jobs," responded Amazon to the Hachette dustup. "Suppliers get to decide the terms under which they are willing to sell to a retailer."

Plus, reports Amazon, Hachette is no mom-and-pop organization, but is rather "part of a $10 billion media conglomerate." On the publishing side of the conglomeration alone, Hachette includes 5 Spot, Back Bay Books, Bulfinch, Business Plus, Center Street, FaithWords, Forever, Grand Central Publishing, Little, Brown & Company, Mulholland Books, Orbit, Reagan Arthur Books, Springboard Press, Twelve, Vision, Wellness Central, and Yen Press in the United States; and Abacus, Atom, Bounty, Business Plus, Cassell, Franklin Watts, Gaia Books, Godsfield, Gollancz, Hamlyn, Headline, Hodder & Stoughton, Hodder Children's, John Murray, Little Black Dress, Little, Brown, Orion, Miller's, Mitchel Beazley, Octopus, Orbit, Orchard, Philip's Phoenix, Piatkus, Sceptre, Sphere, Spruce, Virago, Wayland, and Weidenfeld & Nicolson in the United Kingdom.

Moreover, in spite of their nearly fifty imprints and monstrous size, Hachette represents only 1.1 percent of Amazon's overall sales. In fact, Amazon does "business with more than 70,000 suppliers, including thousands of publishers." A comparison to Amazon is one of the few perspectives from which corporate publishing juggernaut Hachette can appear small.

Hachette, however, does not think that distributive justice is being served by Amazon's tactics. For them, Amazon's actions are no different than the bully tactics of New Jersey's governor. By deliberately slowing or refusing the purchase of titles by Hachette authors such as James Patterson, Steven Colbert, David Foster Wallace, and JK Rowling, Amazon is exercising retributive justice on innocent authors who only want to see their books sell.

According to Hachette's chief executive, Michael Pietsch, the corporation is seeking a deal with Amazon that "best serves our authors and their work, and that preserves our ability to survive . . . as a strong and author-centric publishing company." I'm not sure though that I trust this comment, coming as it does from the editor who was notoriously responsible for the publication of the Frankensteinish final David Foster Wallace novel, *The Pale King*—an editorial project that I regard as one of the low points of contemporary neoliberal corporate publishing.

However, the best defense of the publishing superpower in its dispute with Amazon did not come from Europe's largest publishing group. Rather, it came from one of Hachette Livre's most visible American personalities, the comedian Steven Colbert.

In a recent episode of "The Colbert Report," the satirist memorably skewers Amazon for "deterring customers from buying books by Stephen Colbert."[11] "This is a big blow to my bottom line," jokes Colbert. "That's right, thirty books a year."

But his comedy takes a somewhat uncomfortable turn for bibliophiles when he then attacks Amazon's suggestion that people who need Hachette titles now buy used copies rather than new ones.

"Folks, publishers and authors get no cash from used book sales," comments Colbert. "Plus," he continues, "you don't want them. Used books are the sluts of the literary world. Passed around from person to person. Spreading their pages for anyone. Getting cheaper and cheaper until eventually they end up in prison."

Colbert's jokes here are a painful reminder of several of the recent consequences of both the rise of corporate publishers such as Hachette and the recent success of multinational online distributors such as Amazon.

Recall that the number of independent bookstores has been greatly reduced over the past twenty years—about 2,000 remain today as compared to nearly 7,000 in the mid-nineties—by the rise of bookstore chains such as Borders and Barnes & Noble. This means that even if you wanted to buy a used copy of Colbert's book, you would have a very difficult time finding a bookstore in your area to purchase one.

But the irony here gets even more delicious. These chain bookstores, which helped bring down the independents, have in turn been greatly reduced (Barnes & Noble) or bankrupted (Borders) by the rise of ebooks and online distributors such as Amazon such that even if you wanted to purchase a new copy of Colbert's book at a chain bookstore, you would have a difficult time locating one.

And there is more: these chain bookstores were largely successful because of the advertising deals they struck with large, capital-flush, corporate publishers such as Hachette who rewarded them handsomely to create highly visible displays for some of their mass authors such as James Patterson, Steven Colbert, David Foster Wallace, and JK Rowling. Back in the day, you would walk into a bookstore chain like Borders and almost be attacked by a monster pile of deeply discounted books by an author like Rowling or Patterson.

And now full circle: the big boys with their book monsters were finally brought down by Amazon and other online distributors that afford customers the opportunity to get the books they want (new or used) in the mode they want (ebook or print) at the price they want simply by ordering them by computer or smart phone. By announcing their own version of the smart phone this month, the Amazon Fire, which is said to be especially good for ordering products from Amazon, one can begin to understand how this company has come to control about half of all book sales—and why they are even feared by fellow corporate giants such as Hachette.

But this is the publishing world through the looking glass: a world where it is possible to feel sorry for one of the largest multinational corporate publishing giants in the world—a publishing company that has been ranked as one of the top five largest in the United States and the largest in the United Kingdom.[12]

And it is only through the looking glass of the publishing world that Colbert's biblio-comedy has any purchase for those who despise the ascent of neoliberalism in publishing. The real battle between Amazon and Hachette is not about the discount at which a supplier will provide products to a retailer but rather the price Hachette is willing to pay for Amazon services such as their "pre-order button" and "personalized recommendations" as well as for a "dedicated employee at Amazon for Hachette books." But how different is requesting payment for "pre-order buttons" from paying chain bookstores to set up book monsters in the front of their stores? Not much.

The tables, though, have clearly turned in the book retail business as online retailers such as Amazon clearly now have the upper hand in book distribution as opposed to brick-and-mortar bookstores. Amazon knows that without services like pre-order buttons and employees focused on sales from individual publishers there is a much greater chance that the books they receive from publishers will not sell as well as those from publishers who have these services. This, of course, worries both publishers *and* their authors.

Stephen Colbert's episode continues with an interview with fellow Hachette author Sherman Alexie. "The fortunes of a book are determined before it ever hits the shelves," says Alexie to Colbert. "Pre-publicity and pre-success determine the fortunes of a book," adds Alexie. "So," asks Colbert, "the fact that first-time authors cannot get any pre-sales or orders are delayed is hurting first-time authors?" "The book is dead," responds Alexie.

What Alexie says about pre-sales is a great example of the publishing world as it functions in accordance with the principles of neoliberal economics. For neoliberal publishers, marketing, sales, advertising, and distribution determine the life of a book, not its content. It is a world wherein nothing more than unused or missing pre-order buttons are the difference between literary success and failure.

So who do we root for in a battle like this? A retailer who is willing to intentionally delay e-commerce for economic reasons or a publisher who is unwilling to pay for the retail services that can make its books successful in the world of neoliberal publishing?

Whereas Alexie thinks that to "root for the authors" is to root for Hachette, I'm not so sure. After all, Hachette, along with a handful of other corporate publishers like Penguin Random House, have turned literary value into nothing more than market success—one wherein aesthetics are merely a subset of neoliberal values. Proof of the corporate publishing world's lack of commitment to authors is infallibly demonstrated each time they disinherit authors whose books cease to meet expected sales projections.

It is at this point that the thousands of other publishers that Amazon works with come into play, for it is through online retailers such as Amazon that the works of authors with slow and no sales can persist in perpetuity in the literary marketplace awaiting some reader or critic to discover them. With one or two copies on the shelf in an Amazon warehouse, they always already present authors and their books, particularly those from small and independent press, with hopes of discovery and rediscovery.

While it is true that their tactics with Hachette have more in common with bullying than babying, there is much more in the book world today than the mass-marketed and over-hyped productions of the corporate publishing world, and—for better or worse—Amazon is one of the places that one can discover them.

Let's choose to live in a world where all authors and their books have an opportunity to find their audience. One where books seem as though they live forever. Not one where books are dead if they do not sell well before they are even published.

There may yet be some justice in a publishing world over-run by neoliberal aesthetics and corporate greed—and, all the better, if it results from two corporate giants fighting with each other over pre-order buttons and profit share.

29

Listenin' to the Breeze

"Listen." So begins *Miles: The Autobiography*, with an imperative from the master that no right-minded jazz fan would ignore. Love him or hate him, when Miles Davis spoke to us with his horn, we listened, just as we did when the man behind the horn told his life story back in 1989.

"The greatest feeling I ever had in my life—with my clothes on—was when I first hear Diz and Bird together in St. Louis, back in 1944," he continues. "I was just eighteen years old and had just graduated from Lincoln High School."

Davis's story, like those of Diz and Bird, is part of the origin story of jazz in America, one that cannot be retold enough by its progenitors.

"When I heard Diz and Bird in B's band, I said, 'What? What is this!?' Man, that shit was so terrible it was scary."

It's a moment of pure jazz injected into the teenage bloodstream of a genius. The rest is music history—and Davis left few stones unturned in 400-plus pages of densely and richly packed autobiography.

The jazz world is hyper-competitive, particularly onstage where musicians aim to out-play and out-style one another. It is also a world where the footsteps and shadows of the greats like Bird and Miles are often respected almost to a fault.

This respect is part of the jazz code, a set of unwritten rules. Learning from those who practice them is a revealing glimpse into artistic life. This is the gift of *Benson: The Autobiography* by George Benson and Alan Goldsher: engaging stories from a talented guitarist with a mellow voice who seemed always one step behind the giants of jazz.[13]

George Benson recounts his interactions with and feelings about many musicians from his long and remarkable life in music. In one of the book's more memorable passages, Benson recalls getting a call from Miles asking him to join a recording session. "After I hung up, I stared at the wall for a good long while," says Benson, "the same question blowing through my head over and over again: *What am I going to play on a Miles Davis record?*"

Turns out Benson was right: his role in the session ended up little more than a vamp reinforcement. "And to tell the truth," confesses Benson, "most of what happened that afternoon and evening was *well* out of my comfort zone." But Benson made his mark, laying down the guitar track for "Paraphernalia," a cut from Davis's 1968 classic album, *Miles in the Sky*—a track that opened a new chapter in Davis's musical journey.

Later, Benson recounts getting paired with guitarist John McLaughlin for a gig at Lincoln Center. "I'm sure he [the promoter] was hoping for a guitar gunfight at the O.K. Corral," says Benson. But both guitarists decided to take it back a notch. Afterward, Benson wondered about the strange, sitar-sounding effects used by McLaughlin, who replied, "I don't want people comparing us, so I did something completely different."

Benson is dismissed by some jazz enthusiasts because of his crossover turn toward popular and mainstream music. If anything, Benson's original sin as a jazz musician is becoming a household name. He seems to be aware of this as he tells his story in this wonderfully concise and fast-moving autobiography.

Benson rose in popularity in the mid-1970s with the release of his album *Breezin'*. "After twelve months," writes Benson, "the album sold over four million copies and was nominated for five Grammy Awards." "After that, things started changing. *Drastically.*" But surprisingly, these tales of drastic changes amount to little more than the final thirty-five pages of the book. The fact that Benson devotes only one fifth of the book to the last half of his career, notably the period after he became a household name, is telling. The tension between artistic and commercial success tempers the entirety of his autobiography.

When Benson released *Breezin'*, he was only thirty-three years of age. The album was the result of a recording journey that began back when he was a ten-year-old boy who was driven from Pittsburgh to New York to supposedly sign a record deal. The deal, to be brokered by two young men, one twenty-two and one nineteen, fell through but not before they took "Little Georgie," as he was known back then, to New York City where he auditioned for a couple of shows including *The Arthur Godfrey Show*, who didn't want him because, like Godfrey, he played ukelele.

Six months later, Benson was back in New York City to cut four sides for the RCA Victor Label, including a cover of Nat King Cole's "Mona Lisa." The record, called *Little Georgie Benson: The Kid from Gilmore Alley*, came out on an offshoot RCA label called X. This was the start of a recording journey that would take him to many different labels before ultimately he hit it big with his first album for Warner Brothers Records, *Breezin'*.

The story of his years before the release of *Breezin'* is one of being discovered and rediscovered by people in and around the music industry, including John Hammond, the Columbia Records executive who also discovered Billie Holiday, Count Basie, Big Joe Turner, Teddy Wilson, Benny Goodman, Charlie Christian, Bob Dylan, and Bruce Springsteen.

Hammond discovered Benson gigging in a strip club in the Bronx called the Palm Café. It was 1966, and Benson has just refused an offer from James Brown to be in his house band. Hammond walked into the club, heard one song, and "before he even introduced himself, took a pen from his pocket and a napkin from the table, then he held out both and said, 'Just sign your name here. This is a contract with Columbia Records.'"

But like most of the recording deals Benson signed throughout his life (with the exception of Warner Bros., where he achieved his commercial success), the Columbia deal lasted for only a few years—and then he moved on to other labels (the list here includes Verve, A&M, CTI, GRP, and Concord). A repeated refrain though Benson's life in the music industry involves the challenges of balancing musicianship with commerciality, a theme that will resonate with all artists who struggle to balance innovation with commercial appeal.

Telling Hammond that he wanted to get out of his recording contract with Columbia was not, as you might imagine, an easy one. The book is vague about how he ended the contract (as it is regarding details of other events in his life including run-ins with the law and any aspects of his personal life). However, it does reveal that he asked Hammond, who worked for the biggest record company on the planet, how many records he expected to sell when he signed Benson.

"Somewhere between three thousand and six thousand," said Hammond.

Benson was stunned. He responded, "there's a hundred and eighty million people in America. You mean to tell me that only six thousand of them would want to . . ."

"Listen," Hammond said, "it was nothing to do with you. Even the most famous jazz artists in the world don't move units. Heck, Miles Davis only sells twenty thousand records."

But Benson's album sales would exceed all expectations. Over the course of his career, he has sold millions of albums and won ten Grammy awards. He repeatedly tells us the formula he mastered to balance popularity with musicianship, combining jazz artistry with mass-market music sensibility. He embraced it to the point that now Benson stands for everything that is accessible about jazz music, while Bird his opposite.

Fittingly, the book closes with an anecdote from after one of Benson's shows a few years ago. An older man comes up to him after his concert and praises him for the show. The man says to him, "Mr. Benson, there was one guy from back in the day. He almost destroyed jazz." Benson says to him, "You mean Bird?" The man says, "That's it!"

Benson thought about it and came to the conclusion that the man was right. "He broke the mold," comments Benson about Bird, "but he broke it in a way that enabled those who study his work to put it together in a new, beautiful manner, with a whole new identity, an identity that brought us to where we are now." "And I think we're in a pretty good place."

Of course, Bird didn't destroy jazz. And despite some excellent innovators, it's hard to say that jazz is in a good place these days as we move further away from the primal and formative powers of giants like Bird and Miles. But Benson himself is certainly in a good place, and this book reveals all of the hard work, commitment, and dues he paid to get to there.

Benson is a great storyteller, and this autobiography of a life in jazz will be of interest to anyone who knows what it means to "*listen*."

30

Who Wrote the Last Letter?

Letters are old-school exchange.

The emergence and proliferation of sophisticated communication devices are quietly and decisively bringing to an end a correspondence and literary form that is perhaps as old as writing itself—namely, the letter.

Our new technologically advanced, digitally driven means of formal and informal communication are not only easier to use and quicker to deliver messages than paper and stamp correspondence but also a less expensive and potentially more inclusive means of communication.

An email or a text can be sent by mobile device from any location with cellular service—a task that is generally much easier than locating paper and pen, an address and an envelope, and a stamp and a mailbox. Compared to the time it takes to deliver a letter, the millennial forms of digital communication—email, chat rooms, Facebook, texts, Twitter, Snapchat, blogs, and so on—are instantaneous.

Furthermore, even the most time-intensive of the new forms of communication, such as email and blogs, substantially reduce the delay between correspondence and response, which in turn encourages more correspondence.

While startup costs for millennial communication can be expensive, requiring the purchase a computer or mobile device, the costs are less per communiqué over the lifespan of the device than if the same transactions were enacted by snail mail.

It is at the intersections of cost and ecology that new-school exchange significantly trumps old-school exchange. Imagine the resources required to share the same amount of photos, music, videos, articles, and books via snail mail as opposed to email?

Furthermore, interpersonal communication via the new technology can be much more inclusive. Personal information can be shared easily with multiple people or groups of people, whereas the old technology required much more time and many more resources to achieve the same result.

But unless you actively refuse to take advantage of the new communication technologies—or perhaps live in a cave—none of this is news to you.

Digital communication is the primary form of communication of the new millennium. And while most digital communication can be transferred to paper or be brought into some physical form, who prints out their emails, downloads their MP3 files to CD, or transfers their video files to DVD? Most are content to leave them in electronic purgatory—and have little need or desire to extract them from their digital tomb.

It is in this context that analog correspondence, that is, correspondence like letters that operates outside of the digital universe, is in decline. We are living at a time when the last letter will be—or perhaps already has been—written; a time when it is now possible to ask, "Who wrote the last letter?"

If you think that this is merely speculation or overreaching, ask yourself a couple of questions: First, when was the last time *you* received a personal letter in the mail—let alone by courier? Second, when was the last time you *wrote* a letter? Not a business letter such as a letter of recommendation, but a letter to a friend, colleague, or family member—the kind of correspondence commonly found in a volume of the letters of your favorite writer? One perhaps describing your feelings or emotional state? Or maybe your thoughts on literature, politics, or current events?

A few readers may say "recently;" most will have to travel quite far down memory lane for a response.

As an editor, I still find physical letters in my mailbox, albeit infrequently. Most are requests to review a book or publish a piece. A few are complaints; fewer yet are praise. Most are handwritten or typed, though a few word-processed. Some include a self-addressed stamped envelope that it usually folded over two or three times. The stamps are often offbeat in design, and obviously chosen with care by the correspondent. Regardless of their content, though, these letters always feel dated—as though they are the products of a different era, with more in common with telegrams than Tweets.

Beginning in the mid-nineteenth century, the telegraph allowed communication between distant locations that was faster than ever before. But the development of better and cheaper means of communication rendered the telegraph virtually obsolete by the end of the twentieth-century. (In 1860, a ten-word telegram from New York to New Orleans cost $2.70, about $65 in today's currency, and a transatlantic message to England about $100 or $2,600 today.)

The last commercial electric telegraph system was closed just this past summer. When India's state-run Bharat Sanchar Nigam Ltd. transmitted their last telegrams on July 15, 2013, a mode of communication that had existed for 167 years ceased to be.

The last telegram sent was from an Indian reporter to the Vice President of the Indian National Congress. The reporter, Ashwani Mishra, from India's DD News TV channel, wished Rahul Gandhi, grandson of Indira Gandhi and great grandson of Jawaharlal Nehru, success and happiness in life.

Recognizing the finality of communicating through this medium, Mishra raised the bar in his communiqué by expressing his hope that Gandhi might attain accomplishments in life on a par with other great men of the past.

Will the last letter be of similar flavor? A nostalgic use of the medium tempered with ceremonial gravity? A letter to a world leader, replete with highfalutin sentiments?

At some point, the U.S. Postal Service (USPS) will cease to deliver letters as first-class mail. Will the writer of the last letter delivered by USPS be similarly self-aware of his or her place in history? Will he or she pen a nostalgic nod to a means of communication that can be traced back to the Pony Express, if not to the letters of Cicero—some of which were written with a stylus that cut into wax that was poured over a piece of ivory or wood?

As early as 1977, the USPS recognized that email and other electronic communication would negatively impact first-class mail volume and revenue. To mitigate the impact, they tried to run their own email service. E-COM, as it was called, allowed electronic messages for a fee to be sent to the post office, where they were then printed out and delivered as hard copy.

Though the E-COM experiment was a failure, it did foreshadow the inevitable consequences of digital communication: the decline of physical letters and decreased use of the Postal Service.

I don't believe that the last letter will be written with the intention of being the last letter—though it may be someone's final letter, that is, the last letter that they would ever write.

The last letter will be written by someone who spent a large part of his or her life writing letters—and folding paper into half or thirds.

This last letter has yet to be discovered. It will be the subject of the last chapter of the history of letters, found in a collection written by someone who never corresponded with anyone by email or a text, who spent their life corresponding with others by placing paper in an envelope and affixing it with a stamp.

The last letter will be carried to a mailbox, picked up by a mail carrier and transported to a post office, sorted and routed to its penultimate destination—another post office, where it will be sorted and routed to another carrier to be transported to its final destination—another mailbox. It will be part of the laborious and time-consuming communicative process that dates back to a time when letters were transported by courier or private messenger.

The last letter is a major literary—and historical—artifact.

It will be the object of study and wonder for a generation that has little or no conception of what it means or how it feels to communicate with someone through extended time.

The last letter will be—or perhaps already has been—not only sent but published. It will be found in a collection of letters by a recently deceased author who only corresponded through letters; whose correspondial consciousness has more in common with the letter writers of antiquity than those of cosmodernity.

For this reason, there is heightened excitement in picking up a new collection of letters from a recently deceased author. Could this be the volume that contains the last letter? The companion to the end of an art form?

Sarah Gaddis, William's daughter taunts us when she states that "she never received an email from him, and don't imagine he ever wrote one." Was the last letter written in 1998 by William Gaddis? Is the recently published collection *The Letters of William Gaddis* (2013) the last collection of letters? [14]

These collections mark the passage between one form of communication, consciousness, and identity to another.

In the digital age, we often correspond through images rather than words. Instead of writing about the art exhibit, we send photos of it; instead of describing last night's concert, we send an audio file of it; instead of waiting and reflecting on events and communicating with pen and paper, we correspond in real time about them.

We live in a time of reaction, not reflection; a time of images, not words; and our correspondence demonstrates this difference.

The letter compelled us to form relationships with others under constraints that digital communication does not share. If the only constraint on our current correspondence is cellular service or digital memory or battery life, then the post-letter relational world is very different from the one that occupies the letters of our past.

What this means and how it fundamentally changes our relationships is yet to be determined—and is a notable issue of our time. Letters and letter-writing are important as a tangible marker between pre-digital and digital humanity.

Writing letters after the last letter is an open act of nostalgia. The contemporary letter is correspondence to be marked, a last celebration of paper and of privacy. It's something produced with the full knowledge that its medium is a dead one. The medium does in fact become the message, in that a pen-and-paper letter is a deliberate use of outdated technology, a signifier in itself.

What message is the contemporary letter-writer sending? That the contents of the communication are private, deliberate, considered? That the writer wishes to share not only the distinct voice of her language but the unique angle of the words formed by her hand?

Reading a collection of letters is to travel to a time when correspondence was still an event that forced anticipation and required postage. There is a longevity to these exchanges, the paper objects that were collected and saved by their recipients, that becomes difficult to imagine with contemporary communication. It's hard to envision the widespread anthologizing of email exchanges for the ages. And though comedian Steve Martin may publish his Tweets in hardcover, it's a repackaging of promotion that is already public communication.

The letters in edited collections speak to us about our current shift from private to public communication. They are remnants of an era when singular communications took time to be conveyed and were witnessed by the sender and recipient alone. They bring us not only knowledge of the writers but an understanding of a communicative practice from a time not long ago but already far away.

31

A Sense of the Past

Editing, like baseball, has its mythical past.

But unlike the national pastime, whose myths have been widely circulated and have inspired generations to emulate The Babe or Joltin' Joe DiMaggio, few recognize the figures that appear to transcend the editorial profession.

In 1910, Maxwell Perkins took a job in the advertising department at Charles Scribner's Sons after working as a reporter for *The New York Times*. He rose to prominence by taking on a manuscript that the press's literary advisor, William Crary Brownell, rejected. Brownell, a member of the American Academy of Arts and Letters, objected to Perkins's acquisition of F. Scott Fitzgerald's manuscript *The Romantic Egotist*. However, after working closely with Fitzgerald—and lobbying his colleagues at Scribner's—Perkins saw the work published as *This Side of Paradise* in 1920. The book marked a change in direction for Scribner's, which had been known primarily for publishing eminent writers like John Galsworthy, Henry James, and Edith Wharton. Scribner's would come to be known for ushering in a new generation of writers largely through Perkins' efforts.

Perkins would work on more novels with Fitzgerald, and go on to publish authors including Ernest Hemingway and Thomas Wolfe. He struggled to convince Charles Scribner of the value of Hemingway's *The Sun Also Rises* (1926), particularly due to its profanity. However, Perkins rested all doubts concerning his editorial judgment when Hemingway's next novel, *A Farewell to Arms* (1929), became a number-one best seller. Nonetheless, it was with Wolfe that Perkins found his greatest professional challenge—and established a mythical status for editors.

Wolfe was a prolix writer. His first novel, *Look Homeward, Angel* (1929), was shaped by Perkins, who excised 90,000 words from the text (for perspective, consider that *The Great Gatsby* is only 47,094 words long). With Wolfe's next novel, *Of Time and the River* (1935), Perkins blurred the line between editor and author, turning the three cartons of unnumbered pages and 400,000 words that Wolfe submitted into a novel. In turn, Wolfe explicitly acknowledged Perkins in the book's dedication, calling him "a great editor and a brave and honest man, who stuck to the writer of this book through times of bitter hopelessness and doubt and would not let him give in to his own despair."

One of the results of Perkins-style editing is that the work of the editor in the United States from the '20s to the '40s came to be, in its most distinguished and elite forms, an art in itself. Perkins-style editing involved doing whatever was necessary to support the talents of the author—including taking boxes of raw material and transforming (or translating) them into a finished form. In its most extreme form, editing is seen to be an epic task wherein the editor tirelessly devotes himself or herself to the author. Some see this dedicated, intensive work as admirable; but for others, this type of editing raises serious concerns.

For one, it begs the question as to the authorship of the novel. In the case of *Of Time and the River*, the acknowledged role of Perkins led some critics to question how much Wolfe had actually written. Wolfe himself came to resent the suggestion that he owed his success to Perkins—and Perkins allegedly did not seek or want the publicity that resulted from his "brave" new form of editing. When a work is created under these conditions, does there arise a sense of shared authorship? Is "authorship" reserved for the writer of the original material? How much of the process from blank page to published volume should be the work of the author?

Up until the turn of the nineteenth century, editors spent more time promoting and advocating texts than shaping them. Part of this was due to the fact that up until 1891 British imports had no copyright protection. This meant that the works of, say, Charles Dickens and William Thackeray could be published in the United States with no developmental-, line-, or copy-editing. Furthermore, while "the courtesy of the trade" enabled some British writers to receive a royalty for the American imprints of their work, it was not required by law. For the most part, the task of the editor up until the turn of the century involved directing writers toward lucrative themes, getting them exposure, and composing positive material about their authors for the press that was then presented as objective criticism. Editing, though, started to take its heroic turn at the close of the nineteenth century with the publication of a manuscript that was rejected by numerous publishers.

In 1898, Ripley Hitchcock of Appleton received a manuscript from a banker from upstate New York. Rejected by other publishers, Hitchcock saw potential in Edward Noyes Wescott's *David Harum.* He took the sixth chapter of the book and made it the first chapter, cut some parts, and made stylistic revisions throughout. The result was that *David Harum* was the number-one bestseller of 1899—and, by the time of Maxwell Perkins's death in 1947, had sold over 1.2 million copies. While what Hitchcock did to the manuscript was not unusual for an editor even in the nineteenth century, what was unusual was that people came to know that it was a specific editor's efforts that transformed Wescott's manuscript into a bestseller—and eventually a movie starring Will Rogers.

Though Hitchcock would go on to work with literary giants such as Stephen Crane and Theodore Dreiser, it was his work on *David Harum* that set the stage for the mythic status of the editor. Hitchcock would come to be known as the man who "made" *David Harum* in the same way that Perkins would later come to be known as the man who "made" Fitzgerald, Hemingway, and Wolfe. Editors like Hitchcock and Perkins came to be perceived as individuals who could see what the author envisioned as their final manuscript—and through dedication and diligence were able to bring it into the world as a published novel.

Editors like Hitchcock and Perkins gain their heroic status with the assumption that novels exist in some way in completion even before they are written out or published. The problem with Fitzgerald and Wolfe was not that they did not have finished works, but rather that they were having trouble writing them down accurately. The editor enters in a role similar to a midwife: to assist the author in bringing their novel into the world.

Henry James, who like Fitzgerald and Wolfe, was published by Scribner's, wrote in his notebooks that he was able to "see" his finished novels while in the process of writing them. In *Literature as Conduct: Speech Acts in Henry James* (2005), J. Hillis Miller comments on this with reference to James's unfinished novel, *The Sense of the Past.* Though James died before he was able to finish *The Sense of the Past,* he left extensive notes claiming he could "see" the finished novel. Hillis Miller recounts that James "speaks as if that action has somewhere an ideal existence and his problem is to get access to the already-existing story, so he can write it down correctly, thereby transmitting it to his readers." Hillis Miller compares this "ideal existence" to the ideal object in the work of Edmund Husserl.

"A triangle is for Husserl an ideal mathematical object," says Hillis Miller.

"It exists independently of its actualization in any triangles in the material world." "In a similar way," continues Hillis Miller, "any work of literature, according to Derrida, would exist somewhere, in a perpetual present, even if it were never to get written down, or even if it has been written down but all copies of it have been destroyed."

Hillis Miller's thinking then with regard to James's unfinished manuscript is that it exists finished in a transcendental Husserlian sense, and that the various notes James leaves with regard to it help us to better see it. However, Hillis Miller recommends that we leave unpublished and unfinished work like *The Sense of the Past* in its valuable incompleteness:

> The thing itself, the unwritten part of *The Sense of the Past*, is lost forever. It still exists somewhere as the possibility of the words James did not write. Only James, however, had direct access to that possibility, that virtual reality, that "ideality." With his death, he took his clear vision of *The Sense of the Past* with him to his grave. There it remains encrypted in unrecoverable secrecy, except for the uncanny access without access to it given us by the "Notes."

If one accepts the notion that there are ideal literary objects, then the role of editors is to help authors share their access to this vision. In this model, heroic editors like Hitchcock and Perkins distinguish themselves by their extraordinary ability to coax this ideal object out of their authors. Editors become mythic when they edit or act as though they too have access to their author's ideality.

The myth of the editor as seer of idealities died along with Maxwell Perkins and his generation of editors. The sort of transcendental phenomenology that marked the patience Perkins and his peers had to develop new and emerging authors has little place in the contemporary multinational corporate publishing world.

At least we still have a sense of the past.

32

The Bottom Line

Editors are the midwives of the publishing world. Authors rely on them to strengthen and promote their manuscripts; readers need them to make certain that their limited and valuable reading time is well spent; and publishers depend on their expertise to ensure that their aims are being achieved.

Books benefit from editors in more ways than we know. Developmental and line editors have been rumored to turn lead into gold and a good copy editor is a must for even the most experienced writer. The suggestions made by editors to authors are intended to make books better—and this aim can never be a bad one.

Though most editors labor in anonymity, the work they do does not go unnoticed. As the ultimate handmaidens of the publishing world, the value of editors is relative to their ability to see that the products of the writing process achieve the aims of the publisher, the needs of the reader, and the vision of the author. Even though the author is the star of the publishing show, many authors would not shine as bright were it not for the dedication and hard work of their editors.

However, in spite of the historically large and important role they have played in the publishing world, there is a growing perception that we no longer need editors. For example, many literary agents feign that they have assumed the traditional responsibilities of editors, and have thus left editors with nothing more than ceremonial duties.

Appropriately, Richard Curtis, the New York literary agent and author advocate, once asked Betty Marks, one of his agent colleagues, whether she thought editors were necessary. "Of course they are," quipped Marks. "Who else can take agents to lunch?"

Marks's quip provides but a taste of the general feeling today toward editors. It is one marked by a belief that the age of editors—great and otherwise—has passed, and that what remains is but a shadow of an illustrious past. The editor, namely, the bearer of a particular set of qualities, is slowly disappearing. And this, if anything, is the more charitable description.

The less charitable one is that just like the author, who died many times and in many different ways over the course of twentieth-century theory, the editor too is dead—and also in many different ways.

For my own part, I still believe in the death of the author, which I primarily see as a consequence of the birth of the text, and the significance of the editor, which I experience every day in my own professional practice.

Nevertheless, editors strike me as having fallen by the same sword that killed the author (though I do not know of anyone that has advanced this position).

Regarding discussions of the death of the author, no one is claiming that books just write themselves—and that people like F. Scott Fitzgerald, Ernest Hemingway, and Thomas Wolfe never existed.

Rather, what is generally being asserted is the notion that it does not really mean a whole lot to say that the "author" is responsible for the book, particularly from a critical point of view. As such, the author is not important to textual criticism and aesthetics; instead, what is important is the text.

On the one hand, a classical concept of text allows us to conceive of text as an autonomous object capable of being evaluated in terms of its formal unity, and as integrating various historical, literary, and sociological influences and sources into a new unity.

On the other hand, a contemporary concept of text pushes us to reveal the codes that integrate the text into a whole of signification, and suggests that we view text as a function of linguistic and ideological discourse.

Both directions provide pathways for criticism and aesthetics without what Roland Barthes called the "modern figure" of the "author" produced in the context of the "prestige of the individual."

What then of the "editor"? Is the fate of the editor the same as the fate of the author? Particularly, in light of twentieth-century critical theory—and twenty-first century corporate publishing practice?

As I've said before, the myth of the editor as seer of idealities died along with Maxwell Perkins and his generation of editors. In its shadow has emerged the editor as seer of corporate profits.

The multinational corporate publishing world does not have the patience to develop new and emerging authors the way Perkins and his peers did—that is, through transcendental phenomenology—and many believe this type of editing will never appear again.

Author Harlan Ellison, never one to mince words, addresses this directly: "The Maxwell Perkinses, Walter Fultzes, Ben Hibbses and others are no longer with us, nor will the arena permit their sort to reappear."

Ellison, like many others, attributes the decline of the editor to rise of "multinational corporations obsessed by the bottom line." "Editorial success," comments Ellison, means climbing the corporate ladder," not high levels of daring, intelligence, or even literacy. "Now," claims Ellison, "with editors being drawn from a pool of business school graduates, we find entry-level editorial personnel who are semiliterate and understand debentures better than declensions."

Hyperbole aside, Ellison's point is an accurate one. Corporate publishing demands accountancy skills from its editors, not grammatical or aesthetic prowess. It calls for, spreadsheets, not style sheets. Curtis though argues that "many editorial qualities," such as "taste, discrimination, personal emotional response, a sense of order and organization, determination, devotion, and tender loving care" are irreplaceable. In other words, one can only be an editor if one exhibits these qualities—anything less does not warrant the designation "editor"—not even facility with a spreadsheet.

Yet, within the context of corporate publishing, these qualities are expendable, particularly when they challenge the bottom line. What this means is that corporate publishing now works with "editors" who lack some of the necessary qualities for editing. These corporate editors are but ghosts of their editorial predecessors such as Maxwell Perkins, Walter Fultz, and Ripley Hitchcock. And though Curtis encourages editors who work in corporate publishing not to renounce traditional editorial qualities, it is hard to see how this is a realistic expectation. Editors who fail to follow the bottom line won't have a long shelf life in the corporate publishing world—regardless of whether they exercise the "necessary" attributes of an editor.

For Curtis, the biggest threat to the publishing industry is not corporate mergers, but rather editors who lose their nerve in its presence. "If editors are to remain more than entertaining luncheon hosts," writes Curtis, "if they are to be not merely necessary but indispensible, they will have to continue resisting the pressures toward homogeneity and mediocrity that are arrayed against them by the monolith of Big Publishing." But is this possible? What does Perkins-like editing look like in the world of corporate publishing?

To be sure, it does not involve chasing the rainbow of an author rejected by one's publishing house peers—as well as other publishers. No way Perkins gets to mess with developing a Fitzgerald against the recommendations of his marketing committee—at least not within the context of Big Publishing. However, there are opportunities in corporate publishing to act like a mythic editor who edits as though they have access to authorial idealities. But it is not with new and emerging authors; nor is it even with established ones; rather, if there is any opportunity, it is with distinguished dead authors.

Recall, if you will, editor John F. Callahan's "condensation" of twenty-seven boxes of manuscript into *Juneteenth* (1999), Ralph Ellison's long-awaited second novel, for Vintage Books, a division of Random House, Inc., or editor Michael Pietsch's "completion" of David Foster Wallace's *The Pale King* (2011) for Little, Brown, a part of Hachette Book Group, Inc.

Though the myth of the heroic editor has long since passed, it is resurrected in the corporate publishing world when there is an opportunity to cash in on the prestige of a deceased author. The editor in such cases is charged by the publisher with making a marketable book out of an unfinished manuscript by a major author. Rather than mythic editing, one might more appropriately term it "morgue" editing.

While I philosophically struggle to justify posthumous "condensation" and "completion" of creative works, I still believe there is a place for morgue editing in contemporary letters. However, it is better described by the noun "collection"—rather than "condensation" or "completion." A good example is the publication of *The Original of Laura* in 2009.

According to Dmitri Nabokov, Vladimir's son, his father left unfinished upon his death in 1977 a manuscript consisting of 138 index cards, which amount to about thirty pages of manuscript. Despite the author's directions to destroy any unfinished work upon his death, his wife Vera preserved the notecards but did not publish them. However, after she too died, Dmitri decided to publish the manuscript. The result is 304 pages of reproduced notecards along with transcriptions of them. *Fittingly, the index cards are perforated and can be removed and rearranged, as the author likely did when he was writing the novel.* Fortunately, there is no attempt by the editor to "finish" the novel or express its "ideality." Rather, what was published "reads largely like an outline," writes *Publisher's Weekly*, "full of seeming notes-to-self, references to source material, sentence fragments, commentary and brief flashes of spectacular prose."

The cards themselves are a rare glimpse of the writer as editor at work.

Not only do we see Nabokov's handwriting but also lines that are crossed or blacked out, words that have been added, and copyedit symbols and typesetting notes. For those unfamiliar with the writing and editing process, it is an extraordinary manuscript. It also gives one some perspective on the massive task carried out by Perkins, for example, when he wrestled with three cartons of unnumbered pages and 400,000 words of Wolfe. Just detach the index cards from the book and shuffle them. Now imagine doing this with three *cartons* of cards. Compared to the manuscript of *Of Time and the River*—or even those of Ellison and Wallace—*The Original of Laura* feels like but a footnote.

Arguably, the publication of Nabokov's abandoned manuscript is either the creation of a "literary event" to squeeze a few more bucks out of a great author's legacy or a humbling glimpse of the raw material with which authors and editors work.

Better yet, why not think of it as emblematic of the fate of the editor within the context of corporate publishing. Like the books children adore with their stickers and pop-out features, *The Original of Laura* is something with which to play—you guessed it—mythic editor.

But as you begin to punch out the index cards and rearrange them (channeling your inner Perkins), you gradually work to destroy the (physical) book in your efforts to create the (ideal) book.

Like the sticker book after its stickers are removed, Nabokov's final book is rendered disposable through use—and so too is the notion of the editor as seer of idealities.

Each of us in the act of collecting and collating index cards becomes Nabokov's editor—sorting final lines that his Big Publisher hopes will increase their bottom lines.

The editor is dead—long live the editor—and the bottom line.

33

Don't Fear the Reaper

A lot has been said of late about the death of theory, but not so much on the death of theorists.

Sure, there have been obituaries and legacy volumes—and even some biographies of theorists—but not much discussion about what the deaths of theory's progenitors means for the institution of theory.

In the case of literature, when a major author passes, they are immediately pulled from the contemporary and embalmed in literary history. Their books are often reissued in paperback with fancy new covers—and a volume or two of their letters comes out after a respectful waiting period.

If in life they were more like Rock Stars than Writers, then every last fragment of their estate will be culled for publishable material. The most absurd and sad recent cases are the shameful finishing and exploitative publication of David Foster Wallace's unfinished novel, *The Pale King*, and the publication of few dozen index cards that Vladimir Nabokov was shuffling around into a 280-page "novel in fragments" called *The Original of Laura*.

In short, the marketplace of literature takes care of its dead poets.

But theorists are neither novelists nor poets—let alone the major ones. The work of theory has always been a small-market endeavor—and, in fact, the best-selling books in the field are guidebooks such as Terry Eagleton's *Literary Theory* and anthologies such as Vince Leitch's *Norton Anthology*.

To be sure, even the most well-known and highly regarded theorists only have audiences a fraction of the size of towering literary figures such as Wallace and Nabokov. So, publishing their unfinished and underfinished work posthumously is not a wise marketing decision for presses interested in selling books—that is to say, most solvent presses today. So, even though David Foster

Wallace's master's thesis was published complete with an introductory essay, don't expect Stanley Fish or Barbara Johnson to receive the same treatment.

So, what can we expect? Let's see.

Theory has always struck me as being a *living* entity.

Perhaps it was because its major figures always seemed so full of life and lively—most of all in their writing. Not staid and static creatures like the philosophers, but dynamic and dangerous individuals who by the power of their personalities and enchantment of their intellect brought to life a body of thought that straddled but was never at home in any of the traditional humanities disciplines.

This disciplinary homelessness created a continuous institutional anxiety about theory. Departments who allowed it entry did so at their own peril—a peril fraught with the potential of disrupting their traditional self-identity. But they also opened up their department to a continual sense of new possibilities and knowledge formations as well as to closer ties with other areas of knowledge and academic disciplines.

Through the eyes of theory, traditional disciplinary lines such as philosophy, English, comparative literature, and foreign languages blur via elegant readings that continuously ignore disciplinary stop signs. Moreover, theory always seemed to have a different relationship with history than its associated disciplines.

From the vantage point of theory, the institution of philosophy always appears to be unfolding backward into the call and response of its history, whereas theory always appears to remain in the present—and, in effect, resist the pull of history. It might even be said that efforts to map out "the history" of theory or to capture it "in history" are merely attempts to normalize it, that is, to bring it in line with the histories of more traditional areas of inquiry such as philosophy or science.

Most certainly, when history finally gets a grip on theory it will be history—in the same way that alchemy and philology are history.

But the distinction here is not between the historical and the ahistorical—the drama the institution of philosophy still plays out over and over again; namely, is philosophy a historical or an ahistorical enterprise? Choosing sides here leads to very different types of philosophical discourse. Rather, in the case of theory, the distinction is between the historical and the present—or, more precisely, the contemporary.

For many, to call philosophy *contemporary* is an act of diminishment.

Why? Because philosophers like to believe that their work is either solving problems that transcend time and place or, alternately, that the problems of philosophy are historically situated and contingent. Even today, areas of philosophy that deal with contemporary social and political issues are often viewed within the institution of philosophy as "soft"—philosophy that is more akin to sociology than physics.

However, to call theory *contemporary* has always been a badge of honor. Though the theory of the '60s and '70s did not directly deal with contemporary issues (such as the Vietnam War or the Equal Rights Movement), its anti-establishment approach to the traditional disciplines and formations of knowledge rang well with the progressive politics and political activism of the time. Perhaps it is not a coincidence that the birth of applied ethics within the institution of philosophy in the late '60s and early '70s coincided with the rise of theory—for both are heavily invested in the contemporary.

But the legacies of applied philosophy were never directly linked to the work of particular individuals in the same way that the legacies of theory are linked to their progenitors. And applied philosophy never sought to become interdisciplinary, even though it called upon work in legal studies and sociology.

Applied philosophy took up social and political issues—such as abortion, capital punishment, euthanasia, and animal rights—and read them through the framework of mainstream philosophical analysis. In the United States, this amounted to conceptual analysis and metaethics turned loose on the social and political issues of the day.

Though figures such as Judith Jarvis Thomson from MIT and Peter Singer from Princeton distinguished themselves a bit from the pack of philosophers writing on applied topics, their separation from the rest of the field is not great. And while their contribution to applied ethics will be missed when they die, no one would ever maintain that they will carry applied ethics with them to their grave.

This seems to be the fear though among theorists; namely, that when the last of the great theorists from the final quarter of the twentieth century pass on, so too will theory. The belief seems to be that theory as an institution is not strong enough to withstand the death of its leading figures.

And to some extent there is already some evidence for this in the cases of de Man, Lyotard, Foucault, and Barthes. While their work is still discussed and used (if the sessions of the Modern Language Association or, to a lesser extent, the American Philosophical Association, are any indicator of contemporary relevancy and institutional import), then the work of these folks is already merely history and textbook fodder—or worse.

In the case of de Man, questions about his past continuously threaten to enervate his contemporary status and theoretical legacy. A recent biography by Evelyn Barish, *The Double Life of Paul de Man* (2014), for example, throws gasoline on the de Man character fire by accusing him of forgery, embezzlement, anti-Semitism, bigamy, and Nazi-sympathy among other moral transgressions. Fair or not, even if one is able to regard his theoretical work outside of questions regarding his moral compass, the specter of such questions still haunt his work in same way that they do the work of similarly morally disparaged figures such as Wagner, Pound, and Heidegger.

But what, if anything, died in their theory when they changed tense? Or why does their death seem to coincide with the changing tense of their theory? Why does death seem to have such a profound effect on their legacies, whereas in other new areas of inquiry, such as applied ethics, the death of its major progenitors leaves the area of inquiry virtually unscathed? To be more direct, whereas psychology did not die along with James, Freud, and Lacan, why does theory feel like it is dying with the deaths of Barthes, Foucault, and Derrida?

Perhaps the best answer to questions like these is to be found in the work of theory itself. Just before he died in October of 2004, Jacques Derrida gave what was to be his last interview. Published in the French newspaper *Le Monde*, under the title "I am at war with myself," Derrida said that he was preoccupied with questions of death and inheritance.

"Who is going to inherit, and how?" asked Derrida. "Will there ever be any heirs?"

In some ways, these questions seem odd given the range and impact of his life work. Internationally recognized, widely anthologized, and the author of some seventy books during his lifetime—and many more that have appeared after his death—the last thing on his mind should be inheritance. But it is on his mind—and his response is a beautiful one.

"[W]hen one writes books," reflects Derrida, "you do not know to whom you are speaking, you invent and create silhouettes, but in the end it no longer belongs to you." "Spoken or written," he continues, "all these gestures leave us and begin to act independently of us … [l]ike machines or, better, like marionettes."

"At the moment I leave 'my' book (to be published)," says Derrida, "I become, appearing-disappearing, like that uneducable specter who will have never learned how to live." Derrida continues:

> The trace I leave signifies to me at once my death, either to come or already upon me, and the hope that this trace survives me. This is not a striving for immortality; it's something structural. I leave a piece of paper behind, I go away, I die: it is impossible to escape this structure, it is the unchanging form of my life. Each time I let something go, each time some trace leaves me, 'proceeds' from me, unable to be reappropriated, I live my death in writing.

Issues of the death of theory and the death of theorists (if not also the death of theory editors) are a lot different from Derrida's vantage point. But this will not be news for anyone familiar with his work. "For the written to be the written," wrote Derrida back in 1971, "it must continue to 'act' and to be legible even if what is called the author of the writing no longer answers for what he has written . . . or if he is dead."

Derrida's notion that authors live their death with each book they publish is one to keep in mind amidst consideration of the dual-deaths of theory and theorists. It is also worth remembering that theory continues to "act" even though most of its masters are no longer with us—and some are having their lives and reputations drug through the mud.

Theorists don't fear the reaper.

—In memory of Helen Tartar (1951–2014),
theory editor extraordinaire

34

Experimental Theory

Theory is stronger and more experimental now than it ever was in the twentieth-century. The reason for this is not necessarily a deepening or intensification of the work of theory in traditional areas such as literary criticism and critique (though arguments may be made here), but rather a widening or broadening of its reach and domain.

Theory today is a multi- and interdisciplinary endeavor that operates within and among the humanities (particularly, history, languages, linguistics, the arts, philosophy, and religion, in addition to literature), the social sciences (including anthropology, ethnic and cultural studies, economics, political science, psychology, and sociology), and many of the professions (for example, architecture, business, communication, education, environmental studies, journalism, law, museum studies, media studies, military science, public policy, and sport science, among others).

In addition to its now somewhat more standard-fare work in these areas, of which prime examples are readily available, it has also made some exciting experimental inroads into the natural sciences (for example, biology, physics, the earth sciences, and the space sciences) and the formal sciences (especially mathematics, computer science, and systems science).

To be sure, more disciplines from across the academy have integrated theory into their practice than at any other time in history—and, in many ways, theory today is the id of the disciplines and the experimental engine of interdisciplinary studies.

Moreover, the academic community that engages, supports, and uses theory in the twenty-first century is not only much larger in number than it ever was in the twentieth-century, for many the presumed "heyday of theory," it is also, in part as a consequence of its multi- and interdisciplinary reach, more diverse with respect to the objects and subjects of its attention.

In addition to traditional objects of theoretical engagement, such as literary, philosophical, and artistic texts, many others are now becoming commonplace, such as new media, the environment, and even the university itself.

But theory has also extended the range of *subjects* of its attention. In addition to more commonplace ones such as narrative, identity, translation, and rhetoric, subjects such as affect, globalization, biopolitics, political economy, and institutions have emerged as major areas of experimentation for theory today.

The popularity and strength of theory today is directly related to the experimental fearlessness it engenders in individuals and communities to question the precepts and extend the boundaries of individual disciplines as well as to draw the disciplines into dialogue with each other. In addition, theory's willingness to turn its critical powers upon itself proves to be still another point of attraction. This is why there seems to be nary a subject or object that has not been engaged in some way or another by theory today. To be sure, most everything is fair game for theory's experimentation.

If anything has died in the world of theory in the twenty-first century, then it is the dominance of its "-isms." There was a time in the previous century when affiliation with an "-ism" was the required badge of entry into the theory world. One was not just a "theorist," but a member of a specific subcommunity of theory designated by an "-ism."

Just as the world of religion has Catholicism, Judaism, and Buddhism, the world of theory had structuralism, Marxism, and feminism. And the lines of division between them within the theory community were at times no less flexible than those within the religious community.

Think about how search committees used to badger job candidates with parochial questions about their theoretical affiliation? To do so today almost seems like a violation of FERPA laws. And woe be to the job candidate who professed the wrong theoretical affiliation. Or confessed to the right one, but was not in line with the preferred house of postmodernism or version of feminism?

Though, the late twentieth century may have been the heyday of "high" theory, in retrospect, it appears much more provincial and doctrinaire compared to the contemporary world of theory—one that is not only much more experimental, pluralistic, and amorphous but also less divisive than the previous one.

Whereas in the past, fault lines between and distinctions within "-isms" often became feuding points among theorists, the new object- or subject-centered world of theory is a much less divisive one. Who today is going to argue that the object or subject of your theoretical affection (say, pop music or affect) is the wrong one? Or that working on "debt" is superior to working on "masculinity"? Though there is still some bickering about "who's" debt and "which" masculinity is the right, valid, or true one, such complaints seem more reactionary than progressive, scholastic than pluralistic—and ultimately thus less acceptable—after the demise of the big house of new-, post-, and original flavor "-isms."

Theoretical attention to objects or subjects allows for more experimentation, pluralism, and toleration in the theory-world compared to its previous incarnation as a world of schools, movements, and -isms.

Theory never changed tense, it just changed focus. That is, it just became much more experimental. Since the ascent of high theory (or the even higher, so-called "sky-high theory" or "theoreticism") and the emergence of various forms of opposition to it, rumors of and statements about the demise of theory have persisted. Even today, closure regarding the issue seems remote. Just consider the work of Vincent Leitch, who recently published *Literary Theory in the 21st Century: Theory Renaissance* (2014), one of the most robust and enthusiastic defenses of the continuing presence of theory in the twenty-first century. Leitch acknowledges that word on the street is that theory is dead—superseded by a multitude of studies. Gone are theory stalwarts such as deconstruction, Marxism, and feminism. They have been replaced by studies of everything and anything from Barbie dolls and Beyonce to biopolitics and books.

Leitch's maintains that there are "94 subdisciplines and fields circling around 12 major topics" in literary and cultural theory today, which he notes are "reminiscent of planets and satellites." Of these ninety-four subdisciplines, fifty include adjectives followed by the noun "studies": patronage, subaltern, working-class, debt, object, technoscience, animal, food, postcolonial, border, diaspora, new American, resistance, surveillance and security, body, cyborg, gender, disability, age, leisure, new Southern U.S., Whiteness, indigenous, ethnic, women's, queer, masculinity, sexuality, celebrity, fashion, sport, gaming, sound, visual culture, tv, film, periodical, archive, professionalization, canonization, academic labor, literacy, composition, reception, performance, narrative, trauma, memory, and holocaust.

Another twenty, clearly imply the noun "studies," but for one reason or another it is not stated. For example, the field "media studies" has eight subdisciplines. All but three ("new media," "social media," and "book history") include the noun "studies"—and for at least two of these ("new media" and "social media") the noun "studies" is clearly implied. The final one, "book history," is probably more accurate with "studies" replacing the noun "history." Among the ninety-four subdisciplines, the noun "theory" is only used twice: in "cognitive theory" and "affect theory."

Clearly, if Leitch is even somewhat accurate in his universal mapping of literary and cultural theory in the twenty-first century, there is little or no room in the new millennium for the more dominant mapping of literary theory and criticism, namely, one that divides it into schools and movements. For Leitch, designators of the theory and criticism universe such as Russian formalism, New Criticism, psychoanalysis, feminism, Marxism, structuralism, poststructuralism, queer theory, New Historicism, and postcolonial theory are strictly a twentieth-century phenomena. Though these designators were important to the emergence of "theory" in the last quarter of the twentieth century, they have outlived their usefulness for mapping literary and cultural theory in the twenty-first century. The explosion of "studies" in the first quarter of the twenty-first century leaves little opportunity for organizing literary and cultural theory into the older matrix of schools and movements. Or, alternately stated, studies as subspecies of the "twentieth-century" schools and movements makes for very messy and confusing mapping. Hence, why bother? Better to just leave it to the historians of theory to trace the legacies of theory amidst the "studies" multitude.

What then to do with "theory," that is, the sum body of the twentieth century's schools and movements in the wake of the explosion of twenty-first century studies? Leitch's answer is surprising. Namely, dub the first quarter of the twenty-first century a "theory renaissance." This is the somewhat counterintuitive task of his book—a task that, as difficult as it may sound, is one for which he makes an incredibly strong case. In a nutshell, his argument is that all ninety-four subdisciplines and twelve major topics "stem directly from recognizable contemporary schools and movements of theory." Therefore, because there is no other term that adequately captures the "proliferation" charted into ninety-four subdisciplines and twelve major topics, we need to just continue to use the designator "theory."

Leitch's approach to theory in the twentieth-century is right on the mark and represents the most energetic response to the so-called "death of theory." Not only is theory not dead, it is undergoing a "renaissance," or better yet, a "reinvention," of sorts. To put it bluntly, the death of theory is an illusion—and the future of this illusion, through efforts such as Leitch's, will hopefully be short-lived.

Still, what happens if we replace all of the uses of "study" in his galaxy with the term "theory" and make its implicit references explicit? For one thing, doing so would end the charade that all of these "studies" are not second-generation theory—or dare we say, "*new* theory"? For transitional purposes, it was important at the end of the twentieth century to designate this work with a term other than theory. But a quarter-century later it just seems silly and is confusing, like Prince referring to himself with a symbol. Theory is not dead—it just changed its name when its focus and the objects of its attention began to change and become the subject of broad experimentation.

Calling theory "theory," rather than "studies," allows the larger and committed community dedicated to it to regroup and retool their identity in the wake of major experimentation in the theory world today. It is past time that this was done.

Paraphrasing Mark Twain, "The reports of the death of theory have been greatly exaggerated." Experimental theory represents the best and strongest aspects of theory today. Without it, reports of the death of theory would not be exaggerations.

35

If on a winter's night a computer

Librarians, gaze into the crystal ball and you will see rows of computers—and empty shelves.

The first fully digital public library just opened in Texas.[15] With 150 e-readers, 25 laptops, 25 tablets, but no books, San Antonio now has bragging rights to having launched the first bookless library system in America.

The local judge who launched the library got the idea for it after reading a biography of Steve Jobs, founder of Apple. "If you want to get an idea what it looks like, go into an Apple store," said Bexar County Judge Nelson Wolff.

The library and the commercial retail space are becoming increasingly alike—places lined with screens and busy browsers.

In the late twentieth century, while many took the opportunity to take stock of the state of the book—and to offer prognostications as to its future—novelist and short story writer Italo Calvino chose to refrain.

Given the hyperintensification of change in the world of books, perhaps he was right to not proffer prognostications.

In 1984, Calvino was asked to deliver the Charles Eliot Norton Lectures at Harvard University the following fall. His wife Esther tells us that from the first of the year, "he did practically nothing else" than work on them. He chose the title "Six Memos for the Next Millennium"—and completed writing five of six planned lectures before his untimely death.

Calvino was preparing for his trip from Italy to Cambridge, where he intended to complete writing his final lecture, when he was admitted to a hospital in Sienna. His wife said that he had not yet even packed his lectures. She found them lying in "perfect order" on his writing desk.

Calvino's memos on the art of writing are masterful and provide a lens through which to view his own writing. But what is most interesting about them concerning the futurology of the book is what he chose not to say about it.

He described the millennium that was soon to close as "the millennium of the book, in that it has seen the object we call a book take on the form now familiar to us."

But what he didn't see—or didn't want to see—was that technologies of the book would soon result in major changes for it. "Perhaps it is a sign of our millennium's end," wrote Calvino, "that we frequently wonder what will happen to literature and books in the so-called postindustrial era of technology."

However, although he recognized his lectures as an opportunity to comment on this topic, he said, "I don't much feel like indulging in this sort of speculation." "I'm not here to talk of futurology," continued Calvino, "but of literature."

Fittingly, as Calvino prepared his lectures—and duly avoided talk of futurologies of the book—Steve Jobs was just beginning to lay the groundwork for the future of the book.

In 1984, Apple released the first Macintosh computers. Though these machines were short on memory and could not be upgraded (that is, more like humans than computers) they made up for this by being easy to use, particularly for word processing. With very little training, one could learn to write, save, and print out papers on them.

Calvino had been asked over a decade earlier by IBM to see "how far was it possible to write a story using a computer?" The year was 1973 and Calvino was in Paris when "it wasn't easy to gain access to data processing equipment." The resultant story, "The Burning of the Abominable House," was an example of *ars combinatoria* and "a challenge to his own mathematical abilities."

According to his wife, the story took a great amount of time to complete not because the computer was slow in processing his data—but because he carried out himself "all the operations the computer was supposed to do."

Critic Jonathan Usher traces Calvino's interest with new technology as far back as the late '50s and early '60s when he came to the United States as a recipient of a Ford Foundation grant—and convincingly argues that *If on a winter's night a traveler* represents Calvino's "most developed fictional response to the challenge of the literature machine."

Nonetheless, even though Calvino was clearly intrigued by the possibilities that the computer afford the writer, his ultimate belief was that it is the work of authors to complete the work started by computers—not the opposite.

The future of the book is now directly linked to the development of new technologies but not just those of the word—but also those of global capital.

Follow the technology—and the money—to catch a glimpse of the future of the book.

The U.S. Department of Justice has accused Apple of leading a conspiracy to fix ebook prices. The co-conspirators—Hachette, HarperCollins, Macmillan, Penguin, and Simon & Schuster—have already settled but Apple is still in the crosshairs of the government that claims that it was the leader of this group of six. The smoking gun is apparently an email from Steve Jobs to James Murdoch, former executive vice president of News Corporation.

"Throw in with Apple," wrote Jobs to the son of media mogul Rupert Murdoch, "and see if we can all make a go of this to create a real mainstream ebooks market at $12.99 and $14.99."

This is the same Murdoch who was recently at the center of a phone-hacking scandal involving *News of the World* and News International—a scandal where some 90 people have been arrested and 16 charged with crimes. A report from British Parliament rebuked Murdoch, asserting that he "showed willful ignorance of the extent of the phone-hacking" and was "guilty of an astonishing lack of curiosity" regarding the situation.

News Corporation is the parent company of HarperCollins, the 20th largest book publishing company in the world. Its estimated revenue in 2011 was $1.1 billion—second only to Hachette Livre of the five publishers named in the suit, whose $2.6 billion in revenue made it the 5th largest in the world.

According to the Department of Justice, this group of publishing companies were worried that Amazon's $9.99 Kindle ebook prices were too lean for their diet. So, allegedly, Jobs took the lead in trying to create with them "a real mainstream ebooks market at $12.99 and $14.99."

The publishers, however, have shot back that they are not the monopolists, rather it is Amazon.

Nevertheless, U.S. District Judge Denise L. Cote does not seem to be buying the counternarrative.

"I believe that the government will be able to show at trial direct evidence that Apple knowingly participated in and facilitated a conspiracy to raise prices of ebooks," commented Cote, "and that the circumstantial evidence in this case, including the terms of the agreements, will confirm that."

Calvino's millennial world of the book was one of the possibilities of machine writing, not multinational corporate monopolies—and complete domination of book culture by technology.

His thinking about the relationship of the computer to writing was more along the lines of whether a computer can ever better a person at writing than the total absorption of book culture by the technology industry.

Even Garry Kasparov's loss to Deep Blue was futurology for Calvino. It would be twelve years until a computer beat a reigning world chess champion, that is, until a computer bested a human in a creative endeavor.

No, Calvino's world was one where one still wondered, for example, whether a computer could ever best him in *ars combinatoric* writing—a battle already waged and won by him with IBM in Paris a decade earlier.

Apple's world of iPads, iBooks, iPhones, and iMacs was just emerging in 1984. Its futurologies were on a different order than those of Calvino, namely, on the order of the total absorption of the products of book culture as data—and then their remediation on evolving generations of *iMac*hines.

Apple is now fighting for price points on this data—which is a war with writers distinct from that of "man versus writing machine."

The new millennium has rendered a new form for the book, but we still don't seem any closer to the day when a computer can beat Calvino at writing novels.

36

The Lost Ones

Hemingway's was stolen on a train.

Melville's was last seen in his publisher's office.

And Shakespeare's was last viewed by a king.

Stories and tales about the lost ones—non-extant books by great authors—populate the halls of literary history.

Lost but not forgotten, these books are just as important to the story of Western literature as the ones that have survived.

Remembering the lost ones adds an extra layer of meaning to the books we value. And speculating about them based on the works that remain with us only raises expectations as to what their contribution to literature might have been.

If only Hadley Hemingway had better safeguarded Ernest's handwritten manuscripts, his World War I novel may have seen the light of day. The suitcase that contained the partially completed novel as well as several short stories was stolen on a train from Paris to Switzerland. It was a costly loss for Hadley; Hemingway allegedly divorced her in reaction to the missing manuscripts.

If only Harper and Brothers had not rejected Herman Melville's manuscript *The Isle of the Cross*, we would have his tale of a lighthouse-keeper's daughter who saved and married a shipwrecked sailor—only to be abandoned by him. While the publisher's reason for rejecting the manuscript is unknown, there is speculation that *Isle*, which was based on a true story, opened Harper's to criminal libel if the original persons in Melville's characterizations had been recognized.

There are, of course, many more *if only* claims to American letters—some touched with more mystery and conspiracy than others.

For example, there is the novel Sylvia Plath was working on just before her suicide, and the journals destroyed after her death by her husband, Ted Hughes. While we know by his own admission that Hughes destroyed Plath's last two journals, the fate of her novel is not known. Thirty years after her death, Hughes commented that he was aware of "sixty, seventy pages, which disappeared," and that "he always assumed her mother took them all, on one of her visits."

If only Plath's final novel and journals had remained, how would they add to her literary legacy and speak to her estranged relationship with Hughes?

There are lost works that would not only rewrite their author's legacy but also significantly rewrite literary history.

If only Shakespeare's *Cardenio* had survived, we would have a direct connection between the greatest writer in the English language and the greatest writer in the Spanish language.

Cardenio was a character from Cervantes' *Don Quixote* upon which the Bard and his collaborator, John Fletcher, wrote an entire play. Performed in May of 1613 for King James I, *Cardenio* appeared just a year or so after the English translation of *Quixote*, a translation that would have been available to Shakespeare.

Entire possible literary worlds form around lost ones like *Cardenio.*

What is the shape of a literary world where Shakespeare interacts with Cervantes? Where Shakespearian drama meets the origins of the modern novel?

These missing connections are fertile ground for the imagination. In some ways, it is almost fitting that such a perfect union in literature is not available to us.

Our expectations in all likelihood would probably have exceeded the result.

It is better to tempt our literary imaginations with the possibilities for their narrative union than to actually have them before us. The hypothetical narrative imagination is a powerful one.

Recall Borges's own engagement with Miguel de Cervantes in "Pierre Menard, Author of *Quixote*." "Pierre Menard did not want to compose *another* Quixote, which is surely easy enough," writes Borges, "he wanted to compose *the* Quixote." Might the same be said of Shakespeare? Did he too want to compose *the* Quixote in *Cardenio*?

And then there are the found ones. The recently discovered manuscript by Jamaican American writer and poet Claude McKay, "Amiable With Big Teeth," was never lost because no one knew it even existed. Though research after the discovery of McKay's "Amiable" manuscript verified that he was working on a novel after 1940, the work appears to have been lost and found almost simultaneously.

Something is only lost when its loss is known—and felt. The lost ones gain their power and identity through their continued absence—an absence that is felt by the literary community.

It is an absence that always already holds the promise of something special against a presence that is seldom recoverable.

Yes, there probably were many more books considered for inclusion in the Bible than what we know. However, these books are not the lost ones. Rather, the lost ones are the books that we know were written, but for which no text survives.

Extant passages in the Bible indicate twenty or so specific books that were eliminated from the biblical canon. For example, in the Book of Numbers, the "Book of the Battles of Yahweh" is mentioned. However, no copy survives today.

As such, the Book of the Battles of Yahweh is one of the lost ones. And like all of the lost books of the Bible, it forever holds out the promise of being found—and telling us something new about the books that have survived.

Which begets an ontological question for the lost ones, namely, "What is their relationship to the ones that survived?" Are they in their absence part of their author's *oeuvre* or does their absence give them a different ontological status—say akin to the "gold mountain" or to fiction itself? After all, isn't a lost one a fiction until the point at which it is found?

And of the lost ones relationship to the Bible? Should the books omitted from the Bible be considered "part" of it—or are they simply copy edits?

Ontology quickly begets hermeneutics in considerations of the lost ones.

Perhaps the most tantalizing lost ones are the teasers—those works from which only a few lines survive.

Homer's *Margites* was apparently written before the *Iliad* and the *Odyssey*. This comedic epic poem's hero, Margites, was said by Plato "to know many things, but all badly." However, not much else is known about this epic poem's hero.

If Western literature begins with Homer's *Iliad* and *Odyssey*, what does the specter of a comedic epic poem that preceded it mean for world literature?

Lost books are the undercurrent of literary history—an undercurrent that carries along with it innumerable literary Holy Grails spanning from Homer to Hemingway and from Melville to McKay.

World literature is steeped in *if only*—and the lost ones trace its arc of possibility.

The specter of a book that was once here but is now gone is a powerful one, especially when its author is one that has expanded our sense of what literature is and can be.

With so many ways in the digital world to store and disseminate narrative, it might be argued that everything written today that is worth reading is available to us in one form or another—and that what is lost from here forward was never really worth remembering. That is to say, digital platforms render impossible the notion that our generation will beget lost ones. In fact, our literary plentitude, that is, the massive number of books published each year, raises the notion that not enough of what we produce is lost.

Classical Greek and Roman literature can be contained in its entirety on a pin drive; however, it has been said that just focusing on bestsellers alone, "it would, quantitatively, require three years' hard work to study one year's output conscientiously—even if one could work full time at it."

Too many books renders its own form of absence—an absence felt when we lack the ability to filter our Homers from hogwash . . . or Hogwarts.

Today it seems virtually inconceivable that any significant work from our literary giants will go unpublished—let alone become a lost one. Just look at the David Foster Wallace machine that has not only published his master's thesis but also "finished" his final novel for our reading pleasure. Short of an author destroying or deleting their manuscript, no agent or publisher is going miss an opportunity to publish even the least of their client's work. In this context, the notion of the lost ones itself becomes lost.

AFTERWORD

After *The End of American Literature: Essays from the Late Age of Print*, a Word

by Steve Tomasula

Like letters from a citizen of a country at war with itself, Jeffrey R. Di Leo's dispatches from the country of American literature give an insider's view during a time of upheaval. Rather than delivering polemics, many of his dispatches take the form of spot-on questions: How do the devices we read on affect what is offered for us to read? What are we to make of the fact that the fastest growing segment of publishing is self-published books? Are the humanities in crisis, as one might think from the number of articles in which the word "crisis" features in articles about the humanities, or is it that '"crisis rhetoric" sells papers?" What are the ramifications for literature when the 600-year-old tradition of producing a book and then looking for readers gets turned on its head and publishers instead "sell first, then produce."

As a publisher as well as an editor and critic, much of Di Leo's method is reading the data of books and telling its story: the number of catalogs publishers produce and whether they are mailed in print or emailed digitally; what it means when 63 million ebooks are sold in one year; or the doubling, over a ten-year period, of the number of fiction titles (from 25,000 to 50,000); or how the 30 million books put online by Google compares to the Library of Congress holdings of 37 million volumes. More importantly, the mosaic formed by his essays as a whole gives an impression of the intangible in the way that the best authors on climate change read the data, the histories embedded in ice cores, or the graphs that map the rise in ocean temperatures, before exploring the nonquantifiable consequences for people: for example, how do we measure the loss of "spring time in Paris"? Similarly, Di Leo revisits the passing of independent bookstores at the hands of big-box chains, who were themselves done in by online book selling, and notes the irony of feeling nostalgic for a chain like Barnes and Noble whose business plan to save itself was to "sell more toys." He remembers the pleasure of visiting stores curated by owners and employees who knew books versus stores that were simply treated as boxes to be filled by distributors, and compares Google Books, with its "snippet-only" view to a library that only offers damaged goods. "What happened to book country?" Di Leo asks, from numerous perspectives: from the microlevel of "slow reading" to the macrolevel of "prognostication about capitalism, democracy" and "the coast-to-coast American landscape that used to exist, dotted with bookstores large and small," where "serendipitous readers young and old could get lost for hours hunting through shelves in search of unexpected treasures?" Does the loss of "spring time in Paris" matter for people who have never been to Paris, nor ever intended to go?

Anyone invested in a life of literature has heard similar laments before; indeed, from the very inception of the book, every victory for its democratization has been assailed by the old guard as diminishment. The Gutenberg press dethroned the manuscript Bible as sacred object, and helped spread literacy, transforming reading from the province of its high priests into that of the common congregation, even nonbelievers. And there's a direct evolutionary line from this moment through the rise of power printing presses and cheap paperbacks, to the rise of best sellers, the dominance of pop culture, and ultimately our moment where online publishing —be it in the form of blogs, self-published books, or social platforms like Facebook—has made everyone author-agent-publisher, giving worldwide publishing and distribution tools to neo-Nazis as well as poets. One result, Di Leo writes: "Faster, shorter, and often shriller messages" are most able to cut through the incredible amounts of text we are exposed to with the concomitant result that "focus is given to those who yell." Or, as Marjorie Perloff, one of Di Leo's uber-readers from the age of print puts it, "Never in my own lifetime . . . has 'poetry' been quite as badly written as it is today; never have there been so many 'poets' who are literally talentless and yet win all sorts of prizes and awards and get professorships in good universities."

Rage, rage, against the dying of the light.

And yet, as Di Leo repeatedly reminds us, this time it *is* different or, rather, every time is always different, with the difference that marks our particular moment amplified by the fact that "the past ten years have perhaps been the most transformational ones in the history of the book since the invention of the printing press." Originally written as editorials for the *American Book Review*, perhaps one of the last independent book-review organs (and which is edited by Di Leo), the essays are a kind of consciousness of those tumultuous years: a chronicle of what caught the attention of a publisher, scholar, and critic at the edges of the neoliberal Weltanschauung that so dominates American letters. Comparisons to a journal kept by a samizdat editor during the dominance of Soviet realism would not be too great a stretch in terms of aesthetics, and beliefs in the role literature *can* play in society. Some of the literary objects that caught Di Leo's attention and form the basis for his observations include: the inauguration of the first public library to not have any print books on its shelves; the passing of glorious personal libraries—each a "unique bibliocathedral," built book by book by erudite and creative collectors; the rise of the digital, which allows scholarship to exist only as a Google Chat, followed by the digital fatigue that harbingers the fact that the rumors of the death of print are premature; the economics of book reviewing that promotes "corporate" fiction at the expense of idiosyncratic work; the ever tighter mesh used to track book sales and more closely survey and control publication; the shift in corporate publishing from maximizing profits gleaned from the sale of art to a model that finds and promotes authors and "literature" that will maximize profits; the shift in publishing from editors who achieved success by being daring, intelligent, or literary to those who play it safe as business managers. . . . It's a long, and telling list.

Stepping back from the particulars enough to connect the dots that Di Leo has provided, it's easy to conclude, as does he, that the degree of change we and our book culture are going through is so great as to constitute a difference in kind: it is easy to feel, as did Italo Calvino, that the millennium that had just ended was "the millennium of the book"; that is, that the confluence of economics, culture, technology, book production, and reading habits, gives the sense that all three legs of American Literature—books, literature, and theory—are "going through a period now where many see their best days as behind them."

It was a good, long, run, but now it's done. Or at least done-ish.

For writers like Calvino clearly have a conception of the "book" as a printed object rather than as a textual object. And Di Leo has a symbolic date for the day the age of print ended: November 19, 2007. This is the date that the first Kindle Readers were released by Amazon—and "sold out in four and a half hours." The release of the Kindle marks the end of debates about literature that swung on the differences between paper and electronic books (you can't take it to the beach; reading on screen is like reading text printed on a glowing lightbulb, etc.), as well as the collapse of the divide between paper and electronic books: "Around the same time as the Kindle Reader was released, so too was the mother of all printers," the "Espresso Book Machine" (EBM): an "ATM for books," as it was promoted, which, like the Kindle, could in theory draw on a database of nearly every book ever published anywhere in the world—"in multiple languages, including rare and out of print public domain titles"—and output a printed copy in less time than it took to make an espresso (about four minutes for a book the size of *War and Peace*). Together they made manifest a future where a reader could carry a modern-day library of Alexandria around in his or her pocket. In any case, they would make obsolete the physical infrastructure that had defined book culture for millennium: physical libraries, warehouses of tons of books that were transported by truck to brick-and-mortar stores, and, of course, all the other institutions that kept the system running, including publishing houses, agents, reviewers—the gatekeepers, as Amazon referred to everyone (other than themselves) that stood between the reader and a text. To cite just one marker of how far publishing, literature, and all its corollaries have come, Di Leo offers the publication of *Ulysses* as described in Kevin Birmingham's *The Most Dangerous Book*; he compares the rejections, legal censures, financial straits, world war, and declining health that a literary giant like Joyce had to work through to bring a future classic into the world to the present age where anything can be self-published and distributed worldwide "with ease."

In describing the push-pull between print and pixels, Di Leo returns again and again to the digital infrastructure that underlies not only Kindles and EBMs but our broader cultural transformation as well. As Katherine Hayles reminds us, all books are now digital if their production is taken into account. But the ramifications of this basic fact go far beyond the physical book. A word processor with an internet connection that allows it to surf the web, connect to other books, authors, news feeds, and resources, is not simply an electric pencil. Nor is an eReader simply a book with its ability to "read its reader," that is, to track its readers' reading habits, including which passages, and how fast they read, incorporate audio, merge reader analytics with big-data sale metrics, allow readers to annotate and share passages with others (as well as the companies tracking the reading), and otherwise turn what was once a private, one-to-one experience into "social reading," a very public affair. It's not that "reading," "writing," "publishing" and other terms from the age of print are going away; rather, it's that they are morphing under pressure of the digital with the distinction between *e* and *p* evaporating before our very eyes.

That is, among the ramifications of print and pixels collapsing into one another, one of the largest is that the publishing, sales, and distribution model that has shaped so much of literature up until now is going through its own digital revolution. Up until now, we have lived with parallel worlds: on one hand there was the commercial publishing world that Di Leo identifies, with an ever-shrinking number of players as one publisher was bought up by another, as were the chain bookstores, and mainstream newspaper reviews upon which it depended. In parallel with the neoliberal, commercial print publishing world were the academic, indie, art-house, or small presses that Di Leo was a part of in his role as editor at the *American Book Review*: the presses that, in the balancing act of art and commerce, would always err on the side of art. These were the presses that, for example, published literary magazines and periodicals, like *ABR*, that are not supported by advertising, because in order to attract advertisers, they would have to have the mass-market circulation of the glossy commercial magazines, and to do that, they would have to do what the glossy, commercial magazines do: publish little fiction, practically no poetry, and certainly no innovative or difficult writing of any kind—that is, they would have to lose their reason for being. Virtually all poetry and experimental prose was and is published by the academic-indie-arthouse press. This is a familiar story. What is new is that with the digital revolution, the infrastructure upon which the two publishing worlds were built, and which kept them apart, is now being flattened.

Where will this lead? Di Leo points out the danger of predicting the future by pointing out that a hundred years ago, the most popular movie was D. W. Griffith's *The Birth of a Nation*, an adaptation of the novel *The Clansman: An Historical Romance of the Ku Klux Klan*, and asks us to imagine the reaction an audience in the Black Lives Matter climate of today would have to it. But there is an element of time travel in his advice that to see the future of the book, all one has to do is look at how books—not individual books, but books as a whole—are treated today.

Certainly, the ability to download any book will be a powerful force to make literature more global; but will it come at the expense of making literature more global in the way that McDonalds has made American cuisine more global? A one-book-at-a-time approach to publishing seems to be a force against the current emphasis on blockbuster sales, which is to allow publishing, and so literature, to be more idiosyncratic, more varied, more the way the market for poetry has always been, and the way music has become once it went through its own digital revolution (i.e., a few conglomerates or major labels still dominating bestseller charts even as their share of the total music pie has decreased). That is, in the long view, Di Leo reminds us, there is a dynamic between publishing and literature, with, for example, the backlist of commercial publishers (that is, their older books) becoming part of the long-tail that poetry and experimental prose has always depended on instead of being allowed to quickly go out of print. This leveling seems like a good development for poetry, artist books, experimental or hybrid novels, manuals for build-your-own satellites, and other titles with inherently limited audiences. At least it allows space for idiosyncratic work, works in translation, books that would have been lost under piles of best sellers stacked up in a brick-and-mortar stores of the past, and probably won't make it into the brick-and-mortar stores—or corporate showrooms, as Di Leo calls them—that Amazon envisions as the future, which try to imitate their online progenitors through star ratings by customers (instead of recommendations by knowledgeable curators), and its sales-driven, and sales-driving algorithms.

And perhaps this is the overall moral of *The End of American Literature* and Di Leo's ten years of thinking about books and book culture in the late age of print: the world changes. Our contemporary moment is marked by a degree of interconnectedness, virtual reality, decentralization, heterogeneity, genre (and gene) blurring, surveillance and meta-awareness that would have been difficult for even postmodern thinkers to imagine: the global is literally local, and not just metaphorically so.

Brazilian author Paulo Coelho, who puts his novels online for free and has over four million followers on Twitter, asks those who download one of his books to buy a copy if they like it. The satellites we use to read Coelho's tweets are part of an information network so dense and ubiquitous that it can be used to stage mass protests in Iran and gang fights in Chicago. It allows us to have our taxes prepared by workers in India (at babysitter-scale wages), while the instantaneous and fluid nature of communication Baudrillard ascribed to television is as common as the common newspaper, which is itself globally and instantaneously disseminated, electronic, revised every few minutes.

Algorithms read our habits to recommend movies, books, women, or men we might like to meet, and reading groups interact Facebook-to-Facebook as often as they do face-to-face.

Ultimately, *The End of American Literature* is very much about the material concerns shaping contemporary literature; it is also about the dominant social formations and facts of day-to-day existence, especially reading, that have contributed to a way of reading, thinking, communicating, that is as different in the Late Age of Print as the Modern sense of book culture differed from that of the Medievals. And as Di Leo implies, much of that sense comes from how books come into our hands.

"Who wrote the last letter?" he asks in one of his entries, imagining the day when someone will be the last person to write a letter (I like to imagine with a BIC pen) that the U.S. Postal Service delivers before abandoning the delivery of personal letters (due to lack of interest) as first-class mail. He compares this historic event to the last commercial telegraph, which was sent on July 15, 2013, ending a mode of communication that connected people for 167 years. Like so many of the provocative questions that Di Leo asks in this book, this one begs us to go further, to ask: Who wrote the last novel?—the evolutionary hangover that is a hand-written letter delivered by a mail carrier hauling it in a sack to the home of its intended audience makes us realize that the last novel, as novels were conceived of during the predigital Age of Print, has already been written. Maybe this "major literary—and historical—artifact," as Di Leo says of the last telegram, that marks "the passage from one form of communication, consciousness, and identity to another" has even gone out of print without anyone noticing. What this means, as he says of the last letter, is yet to be determined. The contemporary moment of literature laid out in Jeffrey R. Di Leo's *The End of American Literature* could use Faulkner's famous saying as its epigram: The past is never dead. It's not even past, which is, another way of saying that the future is already here, it just isn't finished.

ACKNOWLEDGMENTS

My primary debt of gratitude goes out to the *American Book Review* and its Reading Series for opening up in more working detail the world of writerly writing and small-press publishing. I could not hope for a better vantage point from which to observe heterodox literature and progressive publishing than from the journal that has been engaged with these matters for now over forty years. It is an honor and privilege to serve as its editor and publisher, and to work with the inspiring company of writers, critics, and publishers that it champions.

All but one of the essays in this volume first appeared in the *American Book Review* from 2013 to 2017. Chapter 19 was previously published in *The Comparatist* 38 (2014) and is used here with permission.

These essays have benefitted from the insightful conversations and timely suggestions of many individuals including Charles Alexander, Frederick Luis Aldama, Charles Bernstein, R. M. Berry, Stephen J. Burn, the late Terry Caesar, Robert Coover, Kwame Dawes, Rikki Ducornet, Brian Evenson, Nick Flynn, Ru Freeman, Robin Truth Goodman, the late Charles B. Harris, Peter Hitchcock, Stephen Graham Jones, Charles Johnson, Michael Joyce, Bill Kartalopolous, Anthony Madrid, Ben Marcus, Carole Maso, Cris Mazza, E. Ethelbert Miller, Paul Allen Miller, Christian Moraru, Warren Motte, Duane Niatum, John O'Brien, Daniel T. O'Hara, Brian O'Keeffe, Marjorie Perloff, Jean Michel Rabaté, Eric Dean Rasmussen, Saba Razvi, Carlin Romano, Jeffrey A. Sartain, Kyle Schlesinger, Nicole Simek, Henry Sussman, Joe Tabbi, Steve Tomasula, John Tytell, and Zahi Zalloua.

A special note of appreciation goes out to Keri Farnsworth and Lauren Pirosko for their editorial support; to Vikki Fitzpatrick and Paula Edging for administrative support; and to the many individuals who have generously supported the American Book Review Endowment.

Finally, I would like to thank my wife, Nina, for her unfailing encouragement, support, and patience.

NOTES

1. Thomas Wolfe, *O Lost: A Story of the Buried Life*, ed. Arlyn Bruccoli and Matthew J. Bruccoli (Columbia: University of South Carolina Press, 2000).
2. Independent bookstore companies: 1,401 (2009); 1,410 (2010); 1,512 (2011); 1,567 (2012); 1,632 (2013); 1,664 (2014); 1,712 (2015); 1,775 (2016). Locations: 1,651 (2009); 1,660 (2010); 1,823 (2011); 1,900 (2012); 1,971 (2013); n/a (2014); 2,227 (2015); 2,311 (2016).
3. Since January of 2008, the University of Rochester has collected figures on the number of translations published in the United States. These figures include ISBN, title, author, translator, publisher, genre, date of publication, gender of author, gender of translator, price, language, and country.
4. Aside from the 28 translations published in 2013 by AmazonCrossing, another 70 or so translations among the 542 were done by corporate publishers or one of their subsidiaries. So, even if we include AmazonCrossing, less than 1 out of 5 translations were done by corporate publishers. Or, alternately stated, 4 out of 5 translations in 2013 were done by small or independent presses.
5. November 21, 2015.
6. See Chapter 20, "Book Machines," for an introduction to the EBM.
7. Kevin Birmingham, *The Most Dangerous Book: The Battle for James Joyce's* Ulysses (New York: The Penguin Press, 2014).
8. Joe Hagan, *Sticky Fingers: The Life and Times of Jann Wenner and* Rolling Stone *Magazine* (New York: Alfred A. Knopf, 2017).
9. Jean-Claude Carrière and Umberto Eco, *This Is Not the End of the Book: A Conversation*, curated by Jean-Philippe de Tonnac, translated from French by Polly McLean (Evanston, IL: Northwestern University Press, 2012).
10. Marjorie Perloff, *Poetics in a New Key: Interviews and Essays*, ed. David Jonathan Y. Bayot (Chicago: University of Chicago Press, 2013).
11. June 3, 2014.
12. In 2007, Hachette Book Group ranked as the fifth largest publisher in the U.S. with sales amounting to 5.3 percent of the total U.S. trade/mass market, and the

largest in the U.K. with sales amounting to 16.6 percent of the total U.K. trade/mass market.

13. George Benson with Alan Goldsher, *Benson: The Autobiography* (Boston: Da Capo Press, 2014).
14. William Gaddis, *The Letters of William Gaddis,* ed. Steven Moore (Champaign: Dalkey Archive, 2013).
15. January 2013.

SOURCES

1. "Saints and Critics." *American Book Review* 38, no. 4 (May/June 2017)
2. "Therapy for the Novel." *American Book Review* 38, no. 6 (September/October 2017)
3. "Slow Philosophy." *American Book Review* 38, no. 5 (July/August 2017)
4. "Publishing Genius." *American Book Review* 38, no. 4 (May/June 2017)
5. "The Writer Who Tried to Save the World." *American Book Review* 38, no. 3 (March/April 2017)
6. "The End of American Literature." *American Book Review* 38, no. 2 (January/February 2017)
7. "Digital Fatigue." *American Book Review* 37, no. 6 (September/October 2016)
8. "The Three Percent." *American Book Review* 37, no. 4 (May/June 2016)
9. "The Corporate Showroom." *American Book Review* 37, no. 5 (July/August 2016):
10. "A Class of His Own." *American Book Review* 37, no. 3 (March/April 2016)
11. "Bootleg Scholarship." *American Book Review* 37, no. 2 (January/February 2016)
12. "3D Printed Man" *American Book Review* 37, no. 1 (November/December 2015)
13. "What's in a Name?" *American Book Review* 36, no. 6 (September/October 2015)
14. "Burn this Book." Review of Kevin Birmingham's *The Most Dangerous Book: The Battle for James Joyce's* Ulysses. *American Book Review* 37, no. 2 (January/February 2016)
15. "Future Readers." *American Book Review* 36, no. 5 (July/August 2015)
16. "The Economics of Book Reviews." *American Book Review* 38, no. 2 (January/February 2017)
17. "Blurbs and Criticism in the Post-Truth Era." *American Book Review* 38, no. 1 (November/December 2016)
18. "Starfucker." Review of Joe Hagan's *Sticky Fingers: The Life and Times of Jann Wenner and* Rolling Stone *Magazine*. *American Book Review* 39, no. 2 (January/February 2018)

19. Review of Umberto Eco and Jean-Claude Carriere's *This Is Not the End of the Book*. *The Comparatist* 38 (2014).

20. "Book Machines." *American Book Review* 35, no. 6 (September/October 2014)

21. "DIY: Self-Publishing in America I." *American Book Review* 36, no. 2 (January/February 2015)

22. "The Boulevard of Broken Dreams: Self-Publishing in America II." *American Book Review* 36, no. 3 (March/April 2015)

23. "Welcome to the Machine: Self-Publishing in America III." *American Book Review* 36, no. 4 (May/June 2015)

24. "Crisis? What Crisis?" *American Book Review* 36, no. 1 (November/December 2014)

25. "How to be a Critic." Review of Marjorie Perloff's *Poetics in a New Key: Interviews and Essays*. Edited by David Jonathan Y. Bayot. *American Book Review* 36, no. 1 (November/December 2014)

26. "The End of Book Country." *American Book Review* 35, no. 5 (July/August 2014)

27. "There is No Success Like Failure." *American Book Review* 35, no. 4 (May/June 2014)

28. "Hardback Justice." *American Book Review* 35, no. 3 (March/April 2014)

29. "Listenin' to the Breeze." Review of George Benson with Alan Goldsher's *Benson: The Autobiography*. *American Book Review* 35, no. 5 (July/August 2014)

30. "Who Wrote the Last Letter?" *American Book Review* 35, no. 1 (November/December 2013)

31. "A Sense of the Past: Editing in America I." *American Book Review* 34, no. 5 (July/August 2013)

32. "The Bottom Line: Editing in America II." *American Book Review* 34, no. 6 (September/October 2013)

33. "Don't Fear the Reaper." *American Book Review* 35, no. 2 (January/February 2014)

34. "Experimental Theory." *American Book Review* 37, no. 5 (July/August 2016)

35. "If on a winter's night a computer." *American Book Review* 34, no. 4 (May/June 2013)

36. "The Lost Ones." *American Book Review* 34, no. 3 (March/April 2013)